True Education

An Adaptation of

Education

By

ELLEN G. WHITE

Pacific Press® Publishing Association
Nampa, Idaho
Oshawa, Ontario, Canada

Designed by Tim Larson
Cover photos © Stan Sinclair and © digital STOCK

Copyright © 2000 by
Pacific Press® Publishing Association
Printed in the United States of America
All Rights Reserved

ISBN 0-8163-1796-8 (Gift Edition)
ISBN 0-8163-1809-3 (ABC/Trade Edition)

00 01 02 03 04 • 5 4 3 2 1

Table of Contents

The Bible as an Educator

Physical Culture

Character Building

The Underteacher

The Higher Course

Foreword

Early in 1903 Ellen G. White published the book *Education*. It was widely circulated and read with appreciation. For decades, the fundamental principles clearly unfolded made it the handbook of tens of thousands of parents and teachers.

Recognizing that nearly one hundred years have passed since this influential book first appeared, and that a new generation is now on the scene, the North American Division Department of Education requested that a special edition be prepared. The present volume, adapted from *Education* and titled *True Education,* is the result. Edited to appeal to the modern mind, we believe it will attract a host of new readers. Unless otherwise indicated, all scripture quotations are from the New King James Version (NKJV) of the Bible, a modern revision of the King James Version, which Mrs. White used most often.

Every person must face the practical realities of life—its opportunities and responsibilities, its successes and its defeats. How one meets these experiences, whether becoming master or victim of circumstances, depends largely on the kind of education one receives.

Many books on the principles and philosophy of education have been published, each one based on a particular core theory as its paradigm. This volume is singularly different in that it flows out of a theological principle that the author calls "the central theme of the Bible" (p. 76). That theme is the "redemption plan, the restoration in the human soul of the image of God" (*ibid.*). In other of her writings, Ellen White describes this core principle as the Great Controversy theme.

Thus, the author points out that "the work of education and the work of redemption are one" (p. 13). With this paradigm in mind, parents and teachers lead students to appreciate that they are "endowed with a power akin to that of the Creator—individuality, power to think and to do." Students who grasp this God-given power are those who "bear responsibilities, . . . are leaders in enterprise, and who influence character. . . . Instead of . . . educated weaklings, . . . [they] are strong to think and to act, . . . masters and not slaves of circumstances, . . . who possess breadth of mind, clearness of thought, and the courage of their convictions" (p. 4).

The motivating objective of the author in her extensive writings on the subject of education was that youth on the threshold of life might be ready to take their place as good citizens, well prepared for the practical experiences of living, fully developed physically, God-fearing, with characters untarnished and hearts true to principle.

Ellen White was a friend of young men and women. She was for many years in close touch with institutions of learning and was well acquainted with the problems of youth in preparation for their lifework. Above all, she was endued with more than ordinary knowledge and skill as a writer and speaker.

Concerned as it is with great principles, and not with the details of curriculum or the merits of differing educational systems, this book, we believe, will have unusual power to guide parents and teachers as they educate today's youth.

Chapter 1

The Source and Aim of True Education

True education means more than pursuing a certain course of study. It has to do with the whole person, and with the whole period of existence possible to human beings. It is the harmonious development of the physical, the mental, and the spiritual powers.

The source of such an education is brought to view in these inspired words that point to the Infinite One: In Him "are hidden all the treasures of wisdom and knowledge." Col. 2:3. The world has had its great teachers, men and women of giant intellect and extensive research, people who have stimulated thought and opened to view vast fields of knowledge. But there is One who stands higher than they. As heavenly bodies in our solar system shine by the reflected light of the sun, so, as far as their teaching is true, do the world's great thinkers reflect the rays of the Sun of Righteousness. Every gleam of thought, every flash of the intellect, is from the Light of the world.

In these days much is said concerning the nature and importance of "higher education." The true "higher education" is that which is imparted by Him out of whose mouth "come knowledge and understanding." Prov. 2:6.

All true knowledge and real development have their source in a knowl-

9

edge of God. Wherever we turn, in the physical, mental, or spiritual realms; in whatever we observe and study, apart from the blight of sin, this knowledge is revealed. Whatever line of investigation we pursue with a sincere purpose to arrive at truth, we are brought in touch with the unseen mighty Intelligence that is working in and through all. The human mind is brought into communion with the mind of God, the finite with the Infinite.

In this communion is found the highest education. It is God's own method of development. "Acquaint yourself with Him" (Job 22:21) is God's message to the human family. The method outlined in these words was the method followed in the education of Adam and Eve.

God's Glorious Purpose

In order to understand what is comprehended in the work of education, we need to consider both the nature of human beings and the purpose of God in creating them. We need to consider also the change in their condition through a knowledge of evil, and God's plan for fulfilling His glorious purpose in the education of the human race.

When Adam and Eve came from the Creator's hand, they bore, in their physical, mental, and spiritual natures, a likeness to their Maker. "God created humankind in His image" (Gen. 1:27, NRSV), and it was His purpose that the longer men and women lived the more fully they should reveal this image. All their faculties were capable of development; their capacity and vigor were continually to increase. Vast was the scope offered for their exercise, glorious the field opened to their research. The mysteries of the visible universe—the "wondrous works of Him who is perfect in knowledge" (Job 37:16)—invited their study. Face-to-face, heart-to-heart communion with their Maker was their high privilege.

If they had remained loyal to God, all this would have been theirs forever. Throughout eternal ages they would have continued to gain new treasures of knowledge, discover fresh springs of happiness, and obtain clearer and yet clearer conceptions of the wisdom, power, and love of God. More and more fully would they have fulfilled the object of their creation, more and more fully would they have reflected the Creator's glory.

But by disobedience this was forfeited. Through sin the divine likeness was marred and almost obliterated. The physical powers of human beings were weakened, their mental capacity was lessened, their spiritual vision was dimmed. They had become subject to death. Yet the race was not left without hope. By infinite love and mercy a life of probation was granted. To restore in men and women the image of their Maker, to bring them back to the perfection in which they were created—this was to be the work of redemption. This is the object of education, the great object of life.

The Place of Love

Love, the basis of creation and of redemption, is the basis of true education. This is made plain in the law that God has given as the guide of life. The first and great commandment is, "You shall love the Lord your God with all your heart, and with all your soul, and with all your strength, and with all your mind." Luke 10:27. To love Him, the infinite, omniscient One, with the whole strength, mind, and heart, means the highest development of every power. It means that the image of God is to be restored in mind and soul.

Like the first is the second commandment—"You shall love your neighbor as yourself." Matt. 22:39. The law of love calls for the devotion of body, mind, and soul to the service of God and humanity. This service, while making us a blessing to others, brings the greatest blessing to ourselves. Unselfishness underlies all true development. Through unselfish service every faculty receives the highest cultivation. More and more fully we become partakers of the divine nature.

Since God is the source of all true knowledge, the first object of education is to direct our minds to His own revelation of Himself. Adam and Eve received knowledge through direct communion with God, and they learned of Him through His works. All created things, in their original perfection, were an expression of the thought of God. To Adam and Eve nature was teeming with divine wisdom. But by transgression the human race was cut off from learning of God through direct communion, and, to a great degree, through His works. The earth, marred and defiled by sin, reflects but dimly the Creator's glory. Nature still speaks of her Creator, yet these revelations are partial and imperfect, and in our fallen state, with weakened powers and restricted vision, we are incapable of interpreting it correctly. We need the fuller revelation of Himself that God has given in His written Word.

The Holy Scriptures are the perfect standard of truth, and as such should be given the highest place in education. To obtain an education worthy of the name, we must receive a knowledge of God, the Creator, and of Christ, the Redeemer, as they are revealed in the sacred Word.

Power to Think and to Do

Every human being, created in the image of God, is endowed with a power akin to that of the Creator—individuality, power to think and to do. The men and women in whom this power is developed are those who bear responsibilities, who are leaders in enterprise, and who influence character. It is the work of true education to develop this power, to train young people to be thinkers, and not mere reflectors of other people's thought. Let students be directed to the sources of truth, to the vast fields opened for research in nature and revelation. Let them contemplate the great facts of duty and destiny, and the mind will expand and strengthen.

Instead of producing educated weaklings, institutions of learning may send forth men and women who are strong to think and act—individuals who are masters and not slaves of circumstances, individuals who possess breadth of mind, clearness of thought, and the courage of their convictions.

Such an education strengthens the character, so that truth and uprightness are not sacrificed to selfish desire or worldly ambition. Instead of some master passion becoming a power to destroy, every motive and desire is brought into conformity to the great principles of right. As the perfection of God's character is dwelt upon, the mind is renewed and the soul is recreated in His image.

What education can be higher than this? What can equal it in value?
"It cannot be gotten for gold,
Neither shall silver be weighed for the price thereof.
It cannot be valued with the gold of Ophir, . . .
For the price of wisdom is above rubies." Job 28:15-18.

God's Ideal for Us

Higher than the highest human thought can reach is God's ideal for His children. Godliness—godlikeness—is the goal to be reached. Before the student there is opened a path of continual progress, an object to achieve, a standard to attain that includes everything good, pure, and noble. Students will advance as fast and as far as possible in every branch of true knowledge. But their efforts will be directed to objects as much higher than mere selfish and temporal interests as the heavens are higher than the earth.

Teachers do a high and noble work by cooperating with the divine purpose in imparting to young people a knowledge of God, and in molding the character in harmony with His. In awaking a desire to reach God's ideal, they present an education that is as high as heaven and as broad as the universe. This education cannot be completed in this life, but will be continued in the life to come. It is an education that secures to successful students a passport from the preparatory school of earth to the higher grade, the school above.

Chapter 2

The Eden School

The system of education instituted at the beginning of the world was to be a model for human beings throughout all time. As an illustration of its principles a model school was established in Eden. The Garden was the schoolroom, nature was the lesson book, the Creator Himself was the instructor, and the parents of the human family were the students.

Created to be "the image and glory of God" (1 Cor. 11:7), Adam and Eve had received endowments worthy of their high destiny. Graceful and symmetrical in form, their countenances glowing with the tint of health and the light of joy and hope, they bore in outward resemblance the likeness of their Maker. Nor was this likeness manifest in the physical nature only. Every faculty of mind and soul reflected the Creator's glory. Adam and Eve were made but "little lower than the angels" (Heb. 2:7) that they might not only discern the wonders of the visible universe but comprehend moral responsibilities and obligations. In the midst of the beautiful scenes of nature untouched by sin, our first parents were to receive their education.

Our heavenly Father personally directed their education. Often they were visited by His messengers, the holy angels, and received counsel and instruction from them. Often as they walked in the garden in the cool of the day they heard the voice of God, and held communion with Him face to face. His thoughts toward them were "thoughts of peace, and not of evil." Jer. 29:11. His every purpose was their highest good.

To Adam and Eve was committed the care of the garden, "to dress it and to keep it." Gen. 2:15. Useful occupation was appointed them as a blessing, to strengthen the body, expand the mind, and develop the character.

The book of nature afforded an exhaustless source of instruction and delight. On every leaf of the forest and stone of the mountains, in every shining star, in earth and sea and sky, God's name was written. With leaf and flower and tree, and with every living creature, the dwellers in Eden held converse, gathering from each the secrets of its life. God's glory in the heavens, the innumerable worlds in their orderly revolutions, "the balancings of the clouds" (Job 37:16), the mysteries of light and sound, of day and night—all were objects of study by the students of earth's first school.

The laws and operations of nature, and the great principles of truth that govern the spiritual universe, were opened to their minds by the infinite Author of all. In "the light of the knowledge of the glory of God" (2 Cor. 4:6), their mental and spiritual powers developed, and they realized the highest pleasures of their holy existence.

As it came from the Creator's hand, not only the Garden of Eden but the whole earth was exceedingly beautiful. No taint of sin or shadow of death marred the fair creation. God's glory "covered the heavens, and the earth was full of His praise." "The morning stars sang together, and all the sons of God shouted for joy." Hab. 3:3; Job 38:7. The earth was a fit emblem of Him who is "abundant in goodness and truth" (Ex. 34:6). It was a fit study for those who were made in His image.

The Garden of Eden was a representation of what God planned that the whole earth would become. It was His purpose that, as the human family increased in numbers, they would establish other homes and schools like the one He had given. Thus in time the whole earth would be occupied with homes and schools where the words and works of God would be studied, and where the students would be fitted more and more fully to reflect, throughout endless ages, the light of the knowledge of His glory.

The Knowledge of Good and Evil

Though created innocent and holy, our first parents were not placed beyond the possibility of wrongdoing. God might have created them without the power to transgress His requirements, but in that case there could have been no development of character. Their service would not have been voluntary, but forced. Therefore He gave them the power of choice—the power to yield or to withhold obedience. And before they could receive fully the blessings He desired to impart, their love and loyalty must be tested.

In the Garden of Eden was the "tree of knowledge of good and evil. . . . And the Lord God commanded the man, saying, 'Of every tree of the garden you may freely eat; but of the tree of the knowledge of good and evil, you shall not eat.'" Gen. 2:9-17. It was the will of God that Adam and Eve should not know evil. The knowledge of good had been freely given them, but the knowledge of sin and its results was in love withheld.

While God was seeking good for the newly created pair, Satan was seeking their ruin. When Eve, disregarding the Lord's admonition concerning the forbidden tree, ventured to approach it, she came into contact with her foe. Her interest and curiosity having been awakened, Satan proceeded to deny God's word and insinuate distrust of His wisdom and goodness. To the woman's statement concerning the tree of knowledge, "God has said, You shall not eat it, nor shall you touch it, lest you die," the tempter answered, "You will not surely die. For God knows that in the day you eat of it your eyes will be opened, and you will be like God, knowing good and evil." Gen. 3:3-5.

Satan tried to make it appear that this knowledge of good mingled with evil would be a blessing, and that in forbidding them to take of the fruit of the tree, God was withholding great good. He urged that it was because of its wonderful properties for imparting wisdom and power that God had forbidden them to taste it, that He was thus seeking to prevent them from reaching a more noble development and finding greater happiness. He declared that he himself had eaten of the forbidden fruit and as a result had acquired the power of speech, and that if they also would eat of it they would attain a more exalted sphere of existence and enter a broader field of knowledge.

While Satan claimed to have received great good by eating of the forbidden tree, he did not let it appear that by transgression he had become an outcast from heaven. Here was falsehood, so concealed under a covering of apparent truth that Eve, infatuated, flattered, beguiled, did not discern the deception. She coveted what God had forbidden, and distrusted His wisdom. She cast away faith, the key of knowledge.

Distrust of God

When Eve saw "that the tree was good for food, and that it was pleasant to the eyes, and a tree desirable to make one wise, she took of its fruit and ate." As she ate, she seemed to feel a vivifying power, and imagined herself entering a higher state of existence. Having herself transgressed, she became a tempter to her husband, "and he ate." Gen. 3:6.

"Your eyes will be opened," the enemy had said, "you will be like God, knowing good and evil." Gen. 3:5. Their eyes were indeed opened, but how sad the opening! The knowledge of evil and the curse of sin were all that the transgressors gained. There was nothing poisonous in the fruit itself, and the sin was not merely in yielding to appetite. It was distrust of God's goodness, disbelief of His word, and rejection of His authority, that made our first parents transgressors and brought into the world a knowledge of evil. It was this that opened the door to every species of falsehood and error.

Our first parents lost all because they chose to listen to the deceiver rather than to Him who alone has understanding. By the mingling of evil with good, their minds became confused, their mental and spiritual powers benumbed. No longer could they appreciate the good that God had so freely bestowed.

Adam and Eve had chosen the knowledge of evil. No longer were they to live in Eden, for in its perfection it could not teach them the lessons it was now essential for them to learn. In unutterable sadness they said goodbye to their beautiful surroundings and went forth to live on the earth, where rested the curse of sin.

To Adam God had said: "Because you have heeded the voice of your wife, and have eaten from the tree of which I commanded you, saying, 'You shall not eat of it': cursed is the ground for your sake; in toil shall you eat of it all the days of your life. Both thorns and thistles it shall bring forth for you, and you shall eat the herb of the field. In the sweat of your face shall you eat bread, till you return to the ground, for out of it you were taken; for dust you are, and to dust you shall return." Gen. 3:17-19.

Although the earth was blighted with the curse, nature was still to be our first parents' lesson book. It could not now represent goodness only, for evil was everywhere present. Where once was written only the character of God—the knowledge of good—was now written also the character of Satan—the knowledge of evil. From nature, which now revealed the knowledge of good and evil, human beings were continually to see the results of sin.

In drooping flower and falling leaf Adam and Eve witnessed the first signs of decay. The stern fact that every living thing must die was brought vividly to their minds. Even the air, on which their life depended, bore the seeds of death.

Continually they were reminded of their lost dominion. Among the lower creatures Adam had stood as king, and so long as he remained loyal to God all nature acknowledged his rule. But when he transgressed, this dominion was forfeited. The spirit of rebellion, to which he himself had given entrance, extended throughout the animal creation. Thus not only the life of humans but the nature of the beasts, the trees of the forest, the grass of the field, even the air—all told the sad lesson of the knowledge of evil.

But the human race was not abandoned to the results of the evil that had been chosen. In the sentence pronounced upon Satan was given an intimation of redemption. "I will put enmity between you and the woman," God said, "and between your seed and her Seed; He shall bruise your head, and you shall bruise His heel." Gen. 3:15. This sentence, spoken in the hearing of our first parents, was to them a promise. Before they heard of the hard work and sorrow that would be theirs, or of the dust to which they must return, they listened to words that gave them hope. All that had been lost by yielding to Satan could be regained through Christ.

Nature repeats this message to us. Though marred by sin, it speaks not only of creation but of redemption. The earth is still rich and beautiful in the tokens of life-giving power. In every manifestation of creative power it holds out the assurance that we may be created anew in "righteousness and true holiness." Eph. 4:24. Thus the very objects and operations of nature that bring vividly to mind our great loss become to us messengers of hope.

As far as evil extends, the voice of our Father is heard, warning His children to forsake the evil and inviting them to receive the good.

Chapter 4

Relation of Education to Redemption

By sin the members of the human family were shut out from God. Without the plan of redemption, eternal separation from God, the darkness of unending night, would have been theirs. But through the Savior's sacrifice, communion with God is again possible. We may not in person approach into His presence and look on His face, but we can see Him and commune with Him in Jesus, the Savior. "The light of the knowledge of the glory of God" is revealed "in the face of Jesus Christ." God is "in Christ, reconciling the world to Himself." 2 Cor. 4:6; 5:19.

"The Word became flesh, and dwelt among us . . . full of grace and truth." "In Him was life, and the life was the light of all people." John 1:14; 1:4, NRSV. The life and death of Christ, the price of our redemption, are not only to us the promise and pledge of life, not only the means of opening again to us the treasures of wisdom, they are a broader, higher revelation of His character than even the holy ones of Eden knew.

And while Christ opens heaven to us, the life that He imparts opens our hearts to heaven. Sin not only shuts us away from God, it destroys in the human soul both the desire and the capacity for knowing Him. Christ's mission is to undo all this work of evil. He has power to invigorate and restore the darkened mind, the perverted will, the faculties of the soul para-

20

lyzed by sin. He opens to us the riches of the universe and imparts the power to discern and appropriate these treasures.

Christ is the "Light, which enlightens everyone." John 1:9, NRSV. As through Christ every human being has life, so also through Him every soul receives some ray of divine light. Not only intellectual but spiritual power, a perception of right, a desire for goodness, exists in every heart. But an antagonistic power is struggling against these principles. The result of eating of the tree of knowledge of good and evil is manifest in every person's experience. There is in our nature a bent to evil, a force which, unaided, we cannot resist. To withstand this force, to attain that ideal which in our inmost soul we accept as alone worthy, we can find help in but one power. That power is Christ. Cooperation with that power is our greatest need. In all educational effort should not this cooperation be our highest aim?

True Teachers Aim to Inspire

True teachers are not satisfied with second-rate work. They are not satisfied with directing their students to a standard lower than it is possible for them to reach. They cannot be content with imparting only technical knowledge, with making merely clever accountants, skillful artisans, successful professionals. It is their ambition to inspire students with principles of truth, obedience, honor, integrity, and purity—principles that will make them a positive force for the stability and uplifting of society. They desire them, above all else, to learn life's great lesson of unselfish service.

These principles become a living power to shape the character, through the acquaintance of the soul with Christ, through an acceptance of His wisdom as the guide, His power as the strength, of heart and life. This union formed, students have found the Source of wisdom. They have within their reach the power to realize their noblest ideals. In the training gained they are entering upon that course which embraces eternity.

In the highest sense the work of education and the work of redemption are one, for in education, as in redemption, "no other foundation can anyone lay than that which is laid, which is Jesus Christ." 1 Cor. 3:11.

Under changed conditions, true education is still conformed to the Creator's plan, the plan of the Eden school. Adam and Eve received instruction through direct communion with God; we behold the light of the knowledge of His glory in the face of Christ.

The great principles of education are unchanged. "They stand fast forever and ever" (Ps. 111:8), for they are the principles of the character of God. To aid the student in comprehending these principles, and in entering into that relation with Christ which will make them a controlling power in the life, should be the teacher's first effort and constant aim. The teacher who accepts this aim is in truth a coworker with Christ, a laborer together with God.

Chapter 5

The Education of Israel

The system of education established in Eden centered in the family. Adam was "the son of God" (Luke 3:38), and it was from their Father that the children of the Highest received instruction. Theirs, in the truest sense, was a family school.

In the divine plan of education as adapted to humanity's condition after the Fall, Christ stands as the representative of the Father, the connecting link between God and the fallen race. He ordained that men and women should be His representatives. The family was the school, the parents were the teachers.

The education centering in the family was that which prevailed in the days of the patriarchs. The people who were under God's direction still pursued the plan of life that He had appointed in the beginning. Those who departed from God built for themselves cities, and, congregating in them, gloried in their splendor, luxury, and vice. But the families who held fast to God's principles lived among the fields and hills. They were tillers of the soil and keepers of flocks and herds. In this free, independent life, with its opportunities for work and study and meditation, they learned of God and taught their children of His works and ways.

This was the method of education that God desired to establish in Israel.

But when brought out of Egypt the parents themselves needed instruction and discipline. Victims of lifelong slavery, they were ignorant, untrained, degraded. They had little knowledge of God and little faith in Him. They were confused by false teaching and corrupted by their long contact with heathenism. God wanted to lift them to a higher moral level, and to this end He endeavored to give them a knowledge of Himself.

In His dealings with the wanderers in the desert, in their exposure to hunger, thirst, and weariness, in their peril from heathen foes, and in the manifestation of His providence for their relief, God was seeking to strengthen their faith by revealing to them the power that was continually working for their good. And having taught them to trust in His love and power, it was His purpose to set before them, in the precepts of His law, the standard of character to which, through His grace, He desired them to attain.

Precious lessons were taught to Israel during their sojourn at Sinai. This was a period of special training, and their surroundings were favorable for accomplishing God's purpose. On the summit of Sinai, overshadowing the plain where the people spread their tents, rested the pillar of cloud that had been the guide of their journey. A pillar of fire by night, it assured them of the divine protection, and while they were locked in slumber, the bread of heaven fell gently upon the encampment. On every hand, vast, rugged heights, in their solemn grandeur, spoke of eternal endurance and majesty. The people were made to feel their ignorance and weakness in the presence of Him who has "weighed the mountains in scales, and the hills in a balance." Isa. 40:12, KJV. Here, by the manifestation of His glory, God endeavored to impress Israel with the holiness of His character and requirements, and the exceeding guilt of transgression.

But the people were slow to learn. Accustomed as they had been in Egypt to material representations of the Deity, and these of the most degrading nature, it was difficult for them to conceive of the existence or the character of the Unseen One. In pity for their weakness, God gave them a symbol of His presence. "Let them make Me a sanctuary," He said, "that I may dwell among them." Exod. 25:8.

In building the sanctuary, Moses was directed to make all things according to the pattern of things in the heavens. God called him into the mount and revealed to him the heavenly things. In their similitude the tabernacle was fashioned.

So to Israel, whom He desired to make His dwelling place, He revealed His glorious ideal of character. The pattern was shown them in the mount when the law was given from Sinai and when God passed by before Moses and proclaimed, "The Lord, the Lord God, merciful and gracious, longsuffering, and abounding in goodness and truth." Exod. 34:6.

But in themselves they were powerless to attain this ideal. The revelation at Sinai could only impress them with their need and helplessness. The tabernacle, through its service of sacrifice, was to teach the lesson of pardon of sin, and power through the Savior for obedience unto life.

Through Christ was to be fulfilled the purpose of which the tabernacle was a symbol—that glorious building, its walls of glistening gold reflecting in rainbow hues the curtains inwrought with cherubim, the fragrance of ever-burning incense pervading all, the priests robed in spotless white, and in the deep mystery of the inner place, above the mercy seat, between the figures of the bowed, worshiping angels, the glory of the Holiest. In all, God desired His people to read His purpose for the human soul. It was the same purpose long afterward set forth by the apostle Paul, speaking by the Holy Spirit: "Do you not know that you are God's temple and that God's spirit dwells in you? If anyone destroys God's temple, God will destroy that person. For God's temple is holy, and you are that temple." 1 Cor. 3:16, 17, NRSV.

A Stupendous Task

Great was the privilege and honor granted Israel in the preparation of the sanctuary; and great also was the responsibility. A structure of surpassing splendor, demanding for its construction the most costly material and the highest artistic skill, was to be erected in the wilderness by a people just escaped from slavery. It seemed a stupendous task. But He who had given the plan of the building stood pledged to cooperate with the builders.

"The Lord spoke to Moses, saying, 'See, I have called by name Bezalel the son of Uri, the son of Hur, of the tribe of Judah. And I have filled him with the Spirit of God, in wisdom, in understanding, and in knowledge, and in all manner of workmanship. . . . And I, indeed I, have appointed with him Aholiab, the son of Ahisamach, of the tribe of Dan; and have put wisdom in the hearts of all the gifted artisans, that they may make all that I have commanded you.'" Exod. 31:1-6.

What a school was that in the wilderness, offering training in industries and having for its instructors Christ and His angels!

All the people were to cooperate in the preparation and furnishing of the sanctuary. There was work for brain and hand. A great variety of material was required, and all were invited to contribute. Thus they were taught to cooperate with God and with one another. And they were to cooperate also in the preparation of the spiritual building—God's temple in the soul.

Even before they left Egypt a temporary organization had been effected, with the people being arranged in companies, under appointed leaders. At Sinai the arrangements for organization were completed. The order so strikingly displayed in all the works of God was manifest in the Hebrew economy. God was the center of authority and government. Moses, as His representative, was to administer the laws in His name. Then came the council of seventy, next the priests and the princes. Under these came "leaders of thousands, leaders of hundreds, leaders of fifties, leaders of tens" (Num. 11:16, 17; Deut. 1:15), and, finally, officers appointed for special duties. The camp was arranged in exact order, the tabernacle as the abiding place of God in the middle, and around it the tents of the priests and Levites. Outside of these each tribe encamped beside its own standard.

Thoroughgoing sanitary regulations were enforced. These were not only necessary to health but were necessary to retain the presence of the Holy One among them. Moses declared to them, "The Lord your God walks in the midst of your camp, to deliver you; . . . therefore your camp shall be holy." Deut. 23:14.

The education of the Israelites included all their habits of life. Everything that concerned their well-being was the subject of divine solicitude. Even in providing food, God sought their highest good. The manna with which He fed them was of a nature to promote physical, mental, and moral strength. Though many of them rebelled against the restriction of their diet, the wisdom of God's choice was vindicated in a manner they could not deny. Notwithstanding the hardships of their wilderness life, there was not a feeble one in all their tribes.

In their journeyings the ark containing the law of God was to lead the way. The place of their encampment was indicated by the descent of the pillar of cloud. As long as the cloud rested over the tabernacle, they remained in camp. When it lifted, they continued their journey. Both the halt and the departure were marked by a solemn invocation. "So it was, whenever the ark set out, that Moses said, 'Rise up, O Lord! Let Your enemies be scattered.' . . . And when it rested, he said: 'Return, O Lord, to the many thousands of Israel.' " Num. 10:35, 36.

Valuable Lessons Taught

As the people journeyed through the wilderness, many precious lessons were fixed in their minds by means of song. At their deliverance from Pharaoh's army the whole host of Israel had joined in the song of triumph. Far over desert and sea rang the joyous refrain, and the mountains re-echoed the accents of praise, "Sing to the Lord, for He has triumphed gloriously!" Exod. 15:21. Often on the journey this song was repeated, cheering the hearts and kindling the faith of the travelers. The commandments as given from Sinai, with promises of God's favor and records of His wonderful works for their deliverance, were by divine direction expressed in song. They were chanted to the sound of instrumental music, and the people kept step as their voices united in praise.

Thus their thoughts were uplifted from the difficulties of the way, the turbulent spirit was calmed, the principles of truth were implanted in the memory, and faith was strengthened. Acting and working together taught order and unity, and the people were brought into closer touch with God and with one another.

Of the dealing of God with Israel during the forty years of wilderness wandering, Moses declared: "As a man chastens his son, so the Lord your God chastens you," "to humble you, and to test you, to know what was in your heart, whether you would keep His commandments or not." Deut. 8:5, 2. "He found him in a desert land, and in the wasteland, a howling wilderness; He encircled him, He instructed him, He kept him as the apple of His eye. As an eagle stirs up its nest, hovers over its young, spreading out its wings, taking them up, carrying them on its wings, so the Lord alone led him, and there was no foreign god with him." Deut. 32:10-12.

God surrounded Israel with every facility, gave them every privilege that would make them an honor to His name and a blessing to surrounding nations. If they would walk in the ways of obedience, He promised to make them "high above all nations which He has made, in praise, in name, and in honor." "All peoples of the earth," He said, "shall see that you are called by the name of the Lord, and they shall be afraid of you." "The peoples who shall hear all these statutes shall say, 'Surely this great nation is a wise and understanding people.'" Deut. 26:19; 28:10; 4:6. In the laws committed to Israel, explicit instruction was given concerning education. To Moses at Sinai God had revealed Himself as "merciful and gracious, longsuffering, and abounding in goodness and truth." Exod. 34:6. The fathers and mothers were to teach these principles to their children. Moses by divine direction declared: "These words which I command you today, shall be in your heart. You shall teach them diligently to your children, and shall talk of them when you sit in your house, when you walk by the way, when you lie down, and when you rise up." Deut. 6:6, 7.

These things were not to be taught as a dry theory. Those who would impart truth must practice its principles themselves. Only by reflecting the character of God in the uprightness, nobility, and unselfishness of their own lives can they impress others.

True education is not forcing instruction on an unready and unreceptive mind. The mental powers must be awakened, the interest aroused. God's method of teaching provided for this. In the home and the sanctuary, through the things of nature and of art, by methods and rites and symbols unnumbered, God gave to Israel lessons illustrating His principles and preserving the memory of His wonderful works. Then, as inquiry was made, the instruction given impressed mind and heart.

In the arrangements for the education of the chosen people it is demonstrated and proved that a life centered in God is a life of completeness. Every desire and drive He has implanted, He provides to satisfy; every faculty imparted, He seeks to develop.

God, the Author of all beauty, Himself a lover of the beautiful, provided to gratify the love of beauty in His children. He made provision also for their social needs, for the kindly and helpful associations that do so much to cultivate sympathy and to brighten and sweeten life.

Education Through Religious Festivals

As a means of education, an important place was filled by the feasts of Israel. In ordinary life the family was both a school and a church, the parents being the instructors in both secular and religious lines. But three times a year seasons were appointed for social exchange and worship, first at Shiloh and afterward at Jerusalem. Only the fathers and sons were required to be present, but none desired to forgo the opportunities of the feasts, hence, so far as possible, all the household were in attendance. With them, as sharers of their hospitality, were the stranger, the Levite, and the poor.

The journey to Jerusalem, in the simple, patriarchal style, amidst the beauty of the springtime, the richness of midsummer, or the ripened glory of autumn, was a delight. With offerings of gratitude they came, from the elderly with white hair to the little child, to meet with God in His holy habitation. As they journeyed, the experiences of the past, the stories that both old and young still love, were recounted to the Hebrew children. The songs that had cheered Israel in their wilderness wandering were sung. God's commandments were chanted, and, bound up with the blessed influences of nature and of kindly human association, they were forever fixed in the memory of many a child and youth.

The ceremonies witnessed at Jerusalem in connection with the paschal service—the night assembly, the men with their girded loins, shoes on feet and staff in hand, the hasty meal, the lamb, the unleavened bread and bitter herbs, and in the solemn silence the rehearsal of the story of the sprinkled blood, the death-dealing angel, and the grand march from the land of bondage—all were of a nature to stir the imagination and impress the heart.

The Feast of Tabernacles, or harvest festival, with its offerings from orchard and field, its week's encampment in the leafy booths, its social reunions, the sacred memorial service, and the generous hospitality to God's workers, the strangers, and the poor, uplifted all minds in gratitude to Him who had crowned the year with His goodness.

By the devout in Israel, fully a month of every year was occupied in this way. It was a period free from care and labor, and almost wholly devoted, in the truest sense, to purposes of education.

Owners of the Land

In apportioning the inheritance of His people, it was God's purpose to teach them, and through them the people of later generations, correct principles concerning ownership of the land. The land of Canaan was divided among the whole people; only the Levites, as ministers of the sanctuary, were excepted. Though a family might for a time dispose of its possession, it could not barter away the inheritance of the children. When able to do so, a person was at liberty at any time to redeem the land; debts were remitted every seventh year, and in the fiftieth, or year of jubilee, all landed property reverted to the original owner. Thus every family was secured in its possession, and a safeguard was afforded against the extremes either of wealth or of poverty.

By the distribution of the land among the people, God provided for them, as for the dwellers in Eden, the occupation most favorable to development—the care of plants and animals. A further provision for education was the suspension of agricultural labor every seventh year, the land lying fallow and its spontaneous products being left to the poor. Thus was given opportunity for more extended study, for social conversation and worship, and for the exercise of benevolence—activities often crowded out by life's cares and labors.

If the principles of God's laws regarding distribution of property were carried out in the world today, how different would be the condition of the people! Observance of these principles would prevent the terrible evils that in all ages have resulted from the oppression of the poor by the rich and the hatred of the rich by the poor. It would aid in bringing a peaceful solution of problems that now threaten to fill the world with anarchy and bloodshed.

The consecration to God of a tithe of all increase, whether of the orchard and harvest field, the flocks and herds, or the labor of brain or hand, the devotion of a second tithe for the relief of the poor and other benevolent uses, tended to keep fresh before the people the truth of God's ownership of all, and of their opportunity to be channels of His blessings. It was a training adapted to kill out selfishness, and to cultivate breadth and nobility of character.

A knowledge of God, fellowship with Him in study and in work, likeness to Him in character, were to be the source, the means, and the aim of Israel's education—the education imparted by God to the parents, and by them to be given to their children.

$\mathcal{C}$ h a p t e r 6

The Schools of the Prophets

Wherever in Israel God's plan of education was carried into effect, the results testified of its Author. But in many households the training appointed by Heaven, and the characters thus developed, were rare. God's plan was but partially and imperfectly fulfilled.

By unbelief and by disregard of the Lord's directions, the Israelites surrounded themselves with temptations that few had power to resist. At their settlement in Canaan "they did not destroy the peoples, concerning whom the Lord had commanded them, but they mingled with the Gentiles and learned their works; they served their idols, which became a snare to them." Their heart was not right with God, "nor were they faithful in His covenant. But He, being full of compassion, forgave their iniquity, and did not destroy them. Yes, many a time He turned His anger away. . . . For He remembered that they were but flesh, a breath that passes away and does not come again." Ps. 106:34-36; 78:37-39.

Fathers and mothers in Israel became indifferent to their obligation to God, indifferent to their obligation to their children. Through unfaithfulness in the home and idolatrous influences around them, many of the Hebrew youth received an education differing widely from that which God had planned for them. They learned the ways of the heathen.

To meet this growing evil, God provided other agencies to aid parents in the work of education. From the earliest times, prophets had been recognized as teachers divinely appointed. In the highest sense the prophet was one who spoke by direct inspiration, communicating to the people the messages received from God. But the name "prophet" was given also to those who, though not so directly inspired, were divinely called to instruct the people in the works and ways of God. For the training of such a class of teachers, Samuel, by the Lord's direction, established the schools of the prophets.

These schools were intended to serve as a barrier against the widespreading corruption, to provide for the mental and spiritual welfare of the youth, and to promote the prosperity of the nation by furnishing it with men qualified to act in the fear of God as leaders and counselors. To this end, Samuel gathered companies of young men who were pious, intelligent, and studious. These were called the sons of the prophets. As they studied the Word and works of God, His life-giving power quickened the energies of mind and soul, and the students received wisdom from above.

The instructors were not only versed in divine truth, they had themselves enjoyed communion with God, and had received the special endowment of His Spirit. They had the respect and confidence of the people, both for learning and for piety. In Samuel's day there were two of these schools—one at Ramah, the home of the prophet, the other at Kirjath-jearim. Later others were established.

The pupils of these schools sustained themselves by their own labor in tilling the soil or in some mechanical employment. Many, also, of the teachers supported themselves by manual labor. In Israel it was regarded as a sin to allow children to grow up in ignorance of useful labor. In Israel it was regarded as a sin to allow children to grow up in ignorance of useful labor.

In both the school and the home much of the teaching was oral, but the youth also learned to read the Hebrew writings, and the parchment rolls of the Old Testament Scriptures were open to their study. The chief subjects of study in these schools were the law of God, with the instruction given to Moses, sacred history, sacred music, and poetry. In the records of sacred history were traced the footsteps of Jehovah. The great truths set forth by the types in the service of the sanctuary were brought to view, and faith grasped the central object of all that system—the Lamb of God, who was to take away the sin of the world. A spirit of devotion was cherished. Not only were the students taught the duty of prayer, they were taught how to pray, how to approach their Creator, how to exercise faith in Him, and how to understand and obey the teachings of His Spirit.

These schools proved to be one of the most effective means in promoting that righteousness which "exalts a nation." Prov. 14:34. In no small degree they aided in laying the foundation of that marvelous prosperity which distinguished the reigns of David and Solomon.

Principles Seen in David's Character

The principles taught in the schools of the prophets were the same that molded David's character and shaped his life. The word of God was his instructor. "Through Your precepts," he said, "I get understanding. . . . I have inclined my heart to perform Your statutes." Ps. 119: 104-112. It was this that caused the Lord to pronounce David "a man after My own heart." Acts 13:22.

In the early life of Solomon also are seen the results of God's method of education. Solomon in his youth made David's choice his own. Above every earthly good he asked of God a wise and understanding heart. And the Lord gave him not only that but riches and honor. The power of his understanding, the extent of his knowledge, the glory of his reign, became the wonder of the world.

In the reigns of David and Solomon, Israel reached the height of its greatness. The promise given to Abraham and repeated through Moses was fulfilled: "If you will diligently observe this entire commandment that I am commanding you, loving the Lord your God, walking in all His ways, and holding fast to Him, then the Lord will drive out all these nations before you, and you will dispossess nations larger and mightier than yourselves. . . . No one will be able to stand against you." Deut. 11:22-25, NRSV.

But in the midst of prosperity lurked danger. The sin of David's later years, though sincerely repented of and severely punished, emboldened the people in transgression of God's commandments. And Solomon's life, after a morning of great promise, was darkened with apostasy. Desire for political power and self-aggrandizement led to alliance with heathen nations. The silver of Tarshish and the gold of Ophir were obtained by sacrificing integrity and betraying sacred trusts. Association with idolaters and marriage with heathen wives corrupted his faith. The barriers that God had set in place for the safety of His people were thus broken down, and Solomon gave himself up to the worship of false gods. On the summit of the Mount of Olives, confronting the temple of Jehovah, were erected gigantic images and altars for the service of heathen deities.

As he cast off his allegiance to God, Solomon lost the mastery of himself. His fine sensibilities became blunted. The conscientious, considerate spirit of his early reign was changed. Pride, ambition, prodigality, and indulgence bore fruit in cruelty and exaction. He who had been a just, compassionate, God-fearing ruler, became tyrannical and oppressive. He who at the dedication of the temple had prayed for his people that their hearts might be undividedly given to the Lord, became their seducer. Solomon dishonored himself, dishonored Israel, and dishonored God.

The nation, of which he had been the pride, followed his leading. Though he afterward repented, his repentance did not prevent a harvest from the evil he had sown. The discipline and training that God appointed for Israel was designed to cause them, in all their ways of life, to differ from the people of other nations. This peculiarity, which should have been regarded as a special privilege and blessing, was to them unwelcome. The simplicity and self-restraint essential to their highest development they longed to exchange for the pomp and self-indulgence of heathen peoples. To be "like all the nations" (1 Sam. 8:5) was their ambition. God's plan of education was set aside, His authority disowned.

The downfall of Israel began in the rejection of God's ways for the ways of heathen contemporaries. It continued until the Jewish people became prey to the very nations whose practices they had chosen to follow.

As a nation the children of Israel failed to receive the benefits that God desired to give them. They did not appreciate His purpose or cooperate in its execution. Though individuals and peoples may separate themselves from Him, His purpose for those who trust Him is unchanged. "Whatever God does, it shall be forever." Eccl. 3:14.

While there are different degrees of development and different manifestations of His power to meet the needs of people in different ages, God's work is forever the same. The Teacher is the same. God's character and His plan are the same. With Him "is no variation or shadow of turning." James 1:17.

The experiences of Israel were recorded for our instruction. "All these things happened to them as examples, and they were written for our admonition, upon whom the ends of the ages have come." 1 Cor. 10:11. With us, as with Israel of old, success in education depends on fidelity in carrying out the Creator's plan. Adherence to the principles of God's Word will bring as great blessings to us as it would have brought to the Hebrew people.

$\mathcal{C}$ h a p t e r 7

Lives of Great Men

Sacred history provides many illustrations of the results of true education. It presents many noble examples of people whose lives were a blessing to others and who stood in the world as representatives of God. Among these are Joseph, Daniel, Moses, Elisha, and Paul.

In early life, just as they were passing from youth to manhood, Joseph and Daniel were separated from their homes and carried as captives to heathen lands. Especially was Joseph subject to the temptations that attend great changes of fortune. In his father's home he was a tenderly cherished child, in the house of Potiphar a slave, in Pharaoh's dungeon a prisoner of state, condemned unjustly. Finally, at a time of great crisis, he was called to leadership in the nation of Egypt. What enabled him to preserve his integrity?

No one can stand on a lofty height without danger. Fierce temptations that leave untouched the lowly in life assail those who stand in the world's high places of success and honor. But Joseph stood both the tests of adversity and of prosperity. The same fidelity was manifest in the palace of the Pharaohs as in the prisoner's cell.

In his childhood, Joseph had been taught the love and fear of God.

Often he had been told the story of the night vision at Bethel, of the ladder from heaven to earth, the descending and ascending angels, and of Him who from the throne above revealed Himself to Jacob. He had been told the story of the conflict beside the Jabbok River, when, renouncing cherished sins, Jacob stood conqueror and received the title of a prince with God.

As a shepherd boy tending his father's flocks, Joseph's pure and simple life had favored the development of both physical and mental power. By communion with God through nature and study of the great truths handed down as a sacred trust from father to son, he had gained strength of mind and firmness of principle.

In the crisis of his life, when making that terrible journey from his childhood home in Canaan to the bondage that awaited him in Egypt, Joseph remembered his father's God. He remembered the lessons of his childhood, and his soul thrilled with the resolve to ever act as a subject of the King of heaven.

In the bitter life of a stranger and a slave, amidst the sights and sounds of vice and the allurements of heathen worship, Joseph was steadfast. He had learned the lesson of obedience to duty.

When he was called to the court of Pharaoh, Egypt was the greatest of nations. In civilization, art, learning, it was unequaled. Through a period of utmost difficulty and danger, Joseph administered the business of the kingdom, and this he did in a manner that won the confidence of the king and the people. Pharaoh "made him lord of his house, and ruler of all his substance: to bind his princes at his pleasure; and teach his senators wisdom." Ps. 105:21, 22.

Inspiration has set the secret of Joseph's life before us. In words of divine power and beauty, Jacob, in the blessing pronounced upon his children, spoke of his best-loved son:

"Joseph is a fruitful bough,
A fruitful bough by a well;
His branches run over the wall.
The archers have bitterly grieved him,
Shot at him and hated him.
But his bow remained in strength,
And the arms of his hands were made strong
By the hands of the mighty God of Jacob." Gen. 49:22-24.

Loyalty to God, faith in the Unseen, was Joseph's anchor. In this lay his power.

Daniel, an Ambassador of Heaven

Daniel and his companions in Babylon were, in their youth, apparently more fortunate than was Joseph in the earlier years of his life in Egypt, yet they were subjected to tests of character scarcely less severe. From the simplicity of their Judean home these youth of royal line were transported to the most magnificent of cities, to the court of its greatest monarch, and were singled out to be trained for the king's special service. Strong temptations surrounded them in that corrupt and luxurious court. The fact that they, the worshipers of Jehovah, were captives to Babylon, that the vessels of God's house had been placed in the temple of the gods of Babylon, that the king of Israel was himself a prisoner in the hands of the Babylonians, was boastfully cited by the victors as evidence that their religion and customs were superior to the religion and customs of the Hebrews. Under such circumstances, through the very humiliations that Israel's departure from His commandments had invited, God gave Babylon evidence of His supremacy, of the holiness of His requirements, and of the sure result of obedience. This testimony He gave through those who still held fast their loyalty.

To Daniel and his companions, at the very outset of their career, came a decisive test. The order that their food should be supplied from the royal table was an expression both of the king's favor and of his interest in their welfare. But a portion of the food had been offered to idols, and by partaking of the king's bounty these young men would be regarded as uniting in homage to false gods. Loyalty to Jehovah forbade them to participate in such homage.

Daniel and his companions had been faithfully instructed in the principles of the Word of God. They had learned to sacrifice the earthly to the spiritual, and they reaped the reward. At the end of their training, in their examination with other candidates for the honors of the kingdom, "none was found like Daniel, Hananiah, Mishael, and Azariah." Dan. 1:19.

At the court of Babylon were gathered talented representatives from all lands, with the highest culture this world could bestow. Yet amidst them all, the Hebrew captives were without a peer. In physical strength and beauty, in mental vigor and literary attainment, they stood unrivaled. "In all matters of wisdom and understanding about which the king examined them, he found them ten times better than all the magicians and astrologers that were in all his realm." Dan. 1:20.

Unwavering in allegiance to God, unyielding in the mastery of himself, Daniel's noble dignity and courteous deference won for him the "favor and tender love" of the heathen officer who was in charge of him. The same characteristics marked all aspects of his life. Soon he rose to the position of prime minister of the kingdom. Throughout the reign of successive monarchs, the downfall of the nation, and the establishment of a rival kingdom, such were his wisdom and statesmanship, so perfect his tact, courtesy, and genuine goodness of heart, combined with fidelity to principle, that even his enemies were forced to say that "they could find no charge or fault, because he was faithful." Dan. 6:4.

While Daniel clung to God with unwavering trust, the spirit of prophetic power came upon him. He was honored by God as His ambassador and taught to read the mysteries of ages to come. Heathen monarchs, through association with Heaven's representative, were constrained to acknowledge the God of Daniel. Nebuchadnezzar declared, "Your God is the God of gods, the Lord of kings, and a revealer of secrets." Dan. 2:47.

True and Honest Men

By their wisdom and justice, by the purity and benevolence of their daily life, by their devotion to the interests of the people, Joseph and Daniel proved themselves true to the principles of their early training, true to Him whose representatives they were. The whole nation honored these men, both in Egypt and in Babylon. In them a heathen people saw an illustration of the goodness and kindness of God, an illustration of the love of Christ.

What a lifework was that of these noble Hebrews! As they bade farewell to their childhood home, little did they dream of their high destiny! Faithful and steadfast, they yielded themselves to divine guidance so that God could fulfill His purpose through them.

The same mighty truths that were revealed through these men, God desires to reveal through young people today.

The greatest want of the world is the want of those men and women who will not be bought or sold, those who in their inmost souls are true and honest, those who do not fear to call sin by its right name, those whose conscience is as true to duty as the needle to the pole, those who will stand for the right though the heavens fall.

But such a character is not the result of accident. It is not due to special favors or endowments of Providence. A noble character is the result of self-discipline, of the subjection of the lower to the higher nature— the surrender of self for the service of love to God and humanity.

Young people need to be impressed with the truth that their endowments are not their own. Strength, time, intellect belong to God, and should be put to the highest use. Youth are branches from which God expects fruit, stewards whose capital must yield increase. Every young person has a work to do for the honor of God and the uplifting of humanity.

Elisha, Faithful in Little Things

The early years of the prophet Elisha were passed in the country, under the teaching of God and nature and the discipline of useful work. In a time of almost universal apostasy his father's household were among those who had not bowed the knee to Baal. Theirs was a home where God was honored and where faithfulness to duty was the rule of daily life.

The son of a wealthy farmer, Elisha possessed the capabilities of a leader. But he received a training in life's common duties. In order to direct wisely, he must learn to obey. By faithfulness in little things, he was prepared for weightier trusts.

Of a meek and gentle spirit, Elisha also possessed energy and steadfastness. He cherished the love and fear of God, and in the humble round of daily toil he gained strength of purpose and nobleness of character, growing in divine grace and knowledge.

The prophetic call came to Elisha while he was plowing in the field. Elijah, divinely directed in seeking a successor, threw his mantle over the young man's shoulders. Elisha recognized and obeyed the summons. He "arose and followed Elijah, and served him." 1 Kings 19:21. No great work was at first required of Elisha. Commonplace duties still constituted his discipline. As the prophet's personal attendant, he continued to prove faithful in little things. With daily strengthening of purpose he devoted himself to the mission appointed by God.

When he was first called, his commitment had been tested. As he turned to follow Elijah he was ordered by the prophet to return home. But Elisha understood the value of his opportunity. Not for any worldly advantage would he forgo the possibility of becoming God's messenger.

As time passed, and Elijah was prepared for translation, so Elisha was prepared to become his successor. And again his faith and commitment were tested. As he accompanied Elijah in his round of service at each place, he was invited by the prophet to turn back. But in his early labor of guiding the plow, Elisha had learned not to fail or become discouraged, and now that he had set his hand to the plow in another line of duty, he would not be diverted from his purpose.

"The two of them stood by the Jordan. Now Elijah took his mantle, rolled it up, and struck the water; and it was divided this way and that, so that the two of them crossed over on dry ground. And so it was, when they had crossed over, that Elijah said to Elisha, 'Ask! What may I do for you, before I am taken away from you?' And Elisha said, 'Please let a double portion of your spirit be upon me.' So he said, 'You have asked a hard thing. Nevertheless, if you see me when I am taken from you, it shall be so for you; but if not, it shall not be so.' Then it happened, as they continued on and talked, that suddenly a chariot of fire appeared with horses of fire, and separated the two of them; and Elijah went up by a whirlwind into heaven.

"Now Elisha saw it, and he cried out, 'My father, my father, the chariot of Israel and its horsemen!' So he saw him no more. And he took hold of his own clothes and tore them into two pieces. He also took up the mantle of Elijah that had fallen from him, and went back and stood by the bank of the Jordan. Then he took the mantle of Elijah that had fallen from him, and struck the water, and said, 'Where is the Lord God of Elijah?' And when he also had struck the water, it was divided this way and that; and Elisha crossed over.

"Now when the sons of the prophets who were from Jericho saw him, they said, 'The spirit of Elijah rests on Elisha.' And they came to meet him, and bowed to the ground before him." 2 Kings 2:6-15.

Henceforth Elisha stood in Elijah's place. And he who had been faithful in that which was least, proved himself faithful also in much.

Elijah, the man of power, had been God's instrument for the overthrow of gigantic evils. The idolatry that had seduced the nation had been cast down. Baal's prophets had been slain. The whole people of Israel had been deeply stirred, and many were returning to the worship of God. A successor to Elijah was needed who by careful, patient instruction could guide Israel in safe paths. Elisha's early training under God's direction had prepared him for this work.

The lesson is for all. None can know what God's purpose in His discipline may be, but all may be certain that faithfulness in little things is the evidence of fitness for greater responsibilities.

Moses, Powerful Through Faith

Moses was younger than Joseph or Daniel when he was removed from the sheltering care of his childhood home, yet the same agencies that shaped their lives molded his. He spent only twelve years with his Hebrew kindred, but during these years the foundation of his greatness was laid.

Jochebed was a slave. Her lot in life was humble, her burden heavy. But through no other woman, except Mary of Nazareth, has the world received greater blessing. Knowing that her child must soon pass beyond her care to the guardianship of those who did not know God, she earnestly endeavored to implant in his heart love and loyalty to God. The work was faithfully accomplished. Nothing could induce Moses to renounce those principles of truth that were the burden of his mother's teaching and the lesson of her life.

From the humble home in Goshen the son of Jochebed passed to the palace of the Pharaohs, to be welcomed by the Egyptian princess. In the schools of Egypt, Moses received the highest civil and military training. Of great personal attractions, noble in form and stature, of cultivated mind and princely bearing, and renowned as a military leader, he became the nation's pride. Moses, though refusing to participate in the heathen worship, was initiated into all the mysteries of the Egyptian religion. As Egypt's prospective sovereign he was heir to the highest honors this world could bestow. But for the honor of God and the deliverance of His downtrodden people, Moses sacrificed the honors of Egypt. Then, in a special sense, God undertook his training.

Not yet was Moses prepared for his lifework. He had yet to learn the lesson of dependence upon divine power. He had mistaken God's purpose. It was his hope to deliver Israel by force of arms. For this he risked all, and failed. In defeat and disappointment he became a fugitive and exile in a strange land.

In the wilds of Midian Moses spent forty years as a keeper of sheep. Apparently cut off forever from his life's mission, he was receiving the discipline essential for its fulfillment. Wisdom to govern an ignorant and undisciplined multitude must be gained through self-mastery. In the care of the sheep and tender lambs he must obtain the experience that would make him a faithful, long-suffering shepherd to Israel. That he might become a representative of God, he must learn of Him.

The influences that had surrounded him in Egypt, the luxury and vice that allured in ten thousand forms, the refinement, the subtlety, and the mysticism of a false religion, had made an impression on his mind and character. In the stern simplicity of the wilderness all this disappeared.

Amidst the solemn majesty of the mountain solitudes Moses was alone with God. Moses seemed to stand in His presence and to be overshadowed by His power. Here his self-sufficiency was swept away. In the presence of the Infinite One he realized how weak, how inefficient, how short-sighted, are mortals.

Here Moses gained a sense of the personal presence of the Divine One. Not merely did he look down the ages for Christ to be made manifest in the flesh, he saw Christ accompanying the host of Israel in all their travels. When misunderstood and misrepresented, he was able to endure "as seeing Him who is invisible." Heb. 11:27.

Moses did not merely think of God, he saw Him. God was the constant vision before him. Never did he lose sight of His face.

To Moses faith was no guesswork, it was a reality. He believed that God ruled his life in particular, and in all its details he acknowledged Him. He felt his need of help, asked for it, by faith grasped it, and in the assurance of sustaining strength went forward.

Such was the experience that Moses gained by his forty years of training in the desert. To impart such an experience, Infinite Wisdom did not count the period too long or the price too great.

The results of that training, of the lessons there taught, are bound up not only with the history of Israel but with all which from that day to this has told for the world's progress. The highest testimony to the greatness of Moses is, "Since then there has not arisen in Israel a prophet like Moses, whom the Lord knew face to face." Deut. 34:10.

Paul, Joyful in Service

With the faith and experience of the Galilean disciples were united the fiery vigor and intellectual power of a rabbi of Jerusalem. A Roman citizen, born in a Gentile city; a Jew, not only by descent but by lifelong training, patriotic devotion, and religious faith; educated in Jerusalem by the most eminent of the rabbis, Saul of Tarsus shared to the fullest extent the pride and prejudices of his nation. While still young, he became an honored member of the Sanhedrin. He was looked upon as a man of promise, a zealous defender of the ancient faith.

In the theological schools of Judea the Word of God had been set aside for human speculations; it was robbed of its power by the interpretations and traditions of the rabbis. The rabbis gloried in their superiority, not only to the people of other nations, but to the masses of their own. With their fierce hatred of their Roman oppressors, they cherished the determination to recover their national supremacy by force of arms. The followers of Jesus, whose message of peace was so contrary to their schemes of ambition, they hated and put to death. In this persecution, Saul was one of the most bitter and relentless actors.

In the military schools of Egypt, Moses was taught the law of force, and so strong a hold did this teaching have on his character that it required forty years of quiet and communion with God and nature to fit him for the leadership of Israel by the law of love. Paul had to learn the same lesson.

At the gate of Damascus the vision of the Crucified One changed the whole current of his life. The persecutor became a disciple, the teacher a learner. The days of darkness spent in solitude at Damascus were as years in his experience. The Old Testament Scriptures stored in his memory were his study, and Christ his teacher. To him also nature's solitudes became a school. To the desert of Arabia he went, there to study the Scriptures and to learn of God. He emptied his soul of prejudices and traditions that had shaped his life, and received instruction from the Source of truth.

The greatest of human teachers, Paul accepted the lowliest as well as the highest duties. He recognized the necessity of labor for the hand as well as for the mind, and he worked at a handicraft for his own support. He pursued his trade of tentmaking while daily preaching the gospel in the great centers of civilization.

While he possessed high intellectual endowments, the life of Paul revealed the power of a rarer wisdom. Principles of deepest import, principles concerning which the greatest minds of this time were ignorant, are unfolded in his teachings and exemplified in his life. Listen to his words before the heathen Lystrians, as he points them to God revealed in nature, the Source of all good, who "gave us rain from heaven and fruitful seasons; filling our hearts with food and gladness." Acts 14:17.

See him in the dungeon at Philippi where, despite his pain-racked body, his song of praise breaks the silence of midnight. After the earthquake opened the prison doors, his voice is heard again in words of cheer to the heathen jailer, "Do yourself no harm, for we are all here" (Acts 16:28). And the jailer, convicted of the reality of that faith which sustains Paul, inquires the way of salvation, and with his whole household unites with the persecuted band of Christ's disciples.

See Paul at Athens before the council of the Areopagus, as he meets science with science, logic with logic, philosophy with philosophy. With the tact born of divine love, he points to Jehovah as "the Unknown God" whom his hearers ignorantly worshiped, and in words quoted from a poet of their own he pictures Him as a Father whose children they are.

Hear him in the court of Festus, when King Agrippa, convicted of the truth of the gospel, exclaims, "You almost persuade me to become a Christian." With what gentle courtesy does Paul, pointing to his own chain, answer, "I would to God, that not only you, but also all who hear me today, might become both almost and altogether such as I am, except these chains." Acts 26:28, 29.

In service he found his joy, and at the close of his life of struggles and triumphs, he could say, "I have fought a good fight." 2 Tim. 4:7.

These histories are of vital interest. To none are they of deeper importance than to young people. Moses renounced a prospective kingdom, and Paul the advantages of wealth and honor among his people. To many the life of these men appears one of renunciation and sacrifice. Was it really so? Moses counted the reproach of Christ greater riches than the treasures in Egypt. Paul declared: "What things were gain to me, these I also counted loss for Christ. But indeed I also count all things loss for the excellence of the knowledge of Christ Jesus my Lord, for whom I have suffered the loss of all things, and count them as rubbish, that I may gain Christ." Phil. 3:7, 8.

Moses was offered the palace of the Pharaohs and the monarch's throne, but the sinful pleasures that make people forget God were in those lordly courts, and he chose instead the "enduring riches and righteousness." Prov. 8:18. Instead of linking himself with the greatness of Egypt, he chose to bind up his life with God's purpose. He became God's instrument in giving to the world those principles that safeguard both the home and society, principles recognized today by the world's greatest thinkers as the foundation of all that is best in human governments.

The greatness of Egypt is in the dust. But the work of Moses can never perish. The great principles of righteousness that he lived to establish are eternal.

Moses' life of toil and heart-burdening care was irradiated with the presence of Him who is "the chiefest among ten thousand" and the One "altogether lovely." Song of Solomon 5:10, 16. His was a life on earth blessing and blessed, and in heaven honored.

Paul also was upheld by the sustaining power of Christ's presence. "I can do all things," he said, "through Christ who strengthens me." Phil. 4:13. Yet there is a future joy to which Paul looked forward as the reward of his labors—the same joy for the sake of which Christ endured the cross and despised the shame—the joy of seeing the result of his work. "What is our hope, or joy, or crown of rejoicing?" he wrote to the Thessalonian converts, "Is it not even you in the presence of our Lord Jesus Christ at His coming? For you are our glory and joy." 1 Thess. 2:19, 20.

Who can measure the results to the world of Paul's lifework? Of all those beneficent influences that alleviate suffering, that comfort sorrow, that restrain evil, that uplift life from the selfish and the sensual and glorify it with the hope of immortality, how much is due to the labors of Paul and his associate workers as with the gospel of the Son of God they made their unnoticed journey from Asia to the shores of Europe?

What is it worth to any life to have been God's instrument in setting in motion such influences of blessing? What will it be worth in eternity to witness the results of such a lifework?

Chapter 8

The Teacher Sent From God

"His name shall be called Wonderful, Counselor, Mighty God, Everlasting Father, Prince of Peace." Isa. 9:6.

In the Teacher sent from God, heaven gave to the human race its best and greatest. He who had stood in the councils of the Most High, who had shared in the innermost sanctuary of the Eternal, was the One chosen to reveal in person the knowledge of God. Through Christ had been communicated every ray of divine light that had ever reached our fallen world. It was He who had spoken through everyone who throughout the ages had declared God's word to mortals. Of Him all the excellencies revealed in the earth's greatest and most noble souls were reflections. In Him was found the perfect ideal.

To reveal this ideal as the only true standard for attainment; to show what every human being may become; what, through the indwelling of humanity by divinity, all who receive Him may become—for this, Christ came to the world. He came to show how the children of God are to be trained, how they are to practice the principles and live the life of heaven.

God's greatest gift was bestowed to meet humanity's greatest need. The Light appeared when the world's darkness was deepest. Through false teaching the minds of men and women had long been turned away from God. In the prevailing systems of education, human philosophy had taken the place of divine revelation. Instead of the heaven-given standard of truth, people had accepted a standard of their own devising. From the Light of life they had turned aside to walk in the sparks of the fire that they had kindled.

Having separated from God, their only dependence being the power of humanity, their strength was but weakness. They were incapable of reaching even the standard set up by themselves. The want of true excellence was supplied by appearance and profession.

From time to time teachers arose who pointed minds to the Source of truth. Right principles were enunciated, and human lives witnessed to their power. But these efforts made no lasting impression. There was a brief check in the current of evil but its downward course was not stayed.

When Christ came to earth, humanity seemed to be fast reaching its lowest point. The very foundations of society were undermined. The Jews, destitute of the power of God's Word, gave to the world mind-benumbing, soul-deadening traditions and speculations. The worship of God "in Spirit and in truth" had been supplanted by the glorification of humans in an endless round of ceremonies. Throughout the world all systems of religion were losing their hold on mind and soul.

As people ceased to recognize the Divine, they ceased to regard the human. Truth, honor, integrity, confidence, compassion, were departing from the earth. Relentless greed and absorbing ambition gave birth to universal distrust. The idea of duty, of the obligation of strength to weakness, of human dignity and human rights, was cast aside as a dream or a fable. Wealth and power, ease and self-indulgence, were sought as the highest good. Physical degeneracy, mental stupor, spiritual death, characterized the age.

As the evil passions and purposes of men and women banished God from their thoughts, so forgetfulness of Him inclined them more strongly to evil. Bent on self-pleasing, they came to regard God as such a one as themselves—a Being whose aim was self-glory, whose requirements were suited to His own pleasure, a Being by whom people were lifted up or cast down according as they helped or hindered His selfish purpose. The lower classes regarded the Supreme Being as one scarcely differing from their oppressors, except by exceeding them in power.

By these ideas every form of religion was molded. Each was a system of requirements. By gifts and ceremonies the worshipers tried to propitiate the Deity in order to secure His favor for their own ends. Evil, unrestrained, grew stronger, while appreciation and desire for good diminished. People lost the image of God and received the impress of the demoniacal power by which they were controlled. The whole world was becoming a sink of corruption.

Only One Hope for the Race

There was but one hope for the human race—that into this mass of discordant and corrupting elements might be introduced a new leaven; that there might be brought to humankind the power of a new life; that the knowledge of God might be restored to the world.

Christ came to restore this knowledge. He came to set aside the false teaching by which those who claimed to know God had misrepresented Him. He came to manifest the nature of His law, to reveal in His own character the beauty of holiness.

Christ came to the world with the accumulated love of eternity. He showed that the law of God is a law of love, an expression of the Divine Goodness. He showed that in obedience to its principles is involved the happiness of everyone, and with it the stability, the very foundation and framework, of human society.

God's law is given as a hedge, a shield. Whoever accepts its principles is preserved from evil. Fidelity to God involves fidelity to humans. Thus the law guards the rights, the individuality, of every human being. It ensures their well-being, both for this world and for the world to come. To the obedient it is the pledge of eternal life, for it expresses the principles that endure forever. Christ came to demonstrate the value of the divine principles by revealing their power for the regeneration of humanity.

With the people of that age the value of all things was determined by outward show. As religion declined in power, it increased in pomp. The educators of the time sought to command respect by display and ostentation. To all this the life of Jesus presented a marked contrast. His life demonstrated the worthlessness of those things that most people regarded as life's great essentials. His education was gained directly from the Heaven-appointed sources—from useful work, from the study of the Scriptures and of nature, and from the experiences of life.

"The Child grew, and became strong in spirit, filled with wisdom; and the grace of God was upon Him." Luke 2:40.

Thus prepared, Jesus went forth to His mission, exerting upon men, women, and children an influence to bless, a power to transform, such as the world had never witnessed.

Anyone who seeks to transform humanity must understand humanity. Only through sympathy, faith, and love can people be reached and uplifted. Here Christ stands revealed as the Master Teacher. He alone has perfect understanding of the human soul.

Christ alone had experience in all the sorrows and temptations that befall human beings. Never was another so fiercely beset by temptation. Never another bore so heavy a burden of the world's sin and pain. Never was there another whose sympathies were so broad or so tender. A sharer in all the experiences of humanity, He could feel not only for, but with, every burdened and tempted and struggling one.

What He taught, He lived. "I have given you an example," He said to His disciples, "that you should do as I have done to you." "I have kept My Father's commandments." John 13:15; 15:10. Thus, in His life Christ's words had perfect illustration and support. And more than this; what He taught, He was. His words were the expression not only of His own life experience but of His own character.

Christ was a faithful reprover. Never lived another who so hated evil, never another whose denunciation of it was so fearless. His very presence was a rebuke to all things untrue and base. In the light of His purity, people saw themselves unclean, their life's aims mean and false. Yet He drew them. He who had created them understood their value. In every human being, however fallen, He saw a child of God, one who might be restored to the privilege of divine relationship.

In every human being He discerned infinite possibilities. He saw people as they might be, transfigured by His grace. Looking upon them with hope, He inspired hope. Meeting them with confidence, He inspired trust. In His presence despised and fallen souls longed to prove themselves worthy of His regard. New impulses were awakened in many a heart that seemed dead to all things holy. To many a despairing one there opened the possibility of a new life.

A Life of Love

Christ bound them to His heart by ties of love and devotion, and by the same ties He bound them to one another. With Him love was life, and life was service. "Freely you have received," He said, "freely give." Matt. 10:8.

It was not on the cross only that Christ sacrificed Himself for humanity. As He "went about doing good" (Acts 10:38), every day's experience was an outpouring of His life. In one way only could such a life be sustained. Jesus lived in dependence upon God and communion with Him. His life was one of constant trust, sustained by continual communion, and His service for heaven and earth was without failure or faltering.

As a man Jesus supplicated the throne of God till His humanity was charged with a heavenly current that connected humanity with divinity. Receiving life from God, He imparted life to others.

Instead of directing the people to study human theories about God, His Word, or His works, He taught them to behold Him, as manifested in His works, in His Word, and by His providences. He brought their minds into contact with the mind of the Infinite.

"No man ever spoke like this Man." John 7:46. This would have been true of Christ if He had taught only in the area of the physical and intellectual, or only in matters of theory and speculation. He might have unlocked mysteries that have taken centuries of work and study to solve. He might have made suggestions in scientific matters that would have stimulated thought and invention till the close of time. But He did not do this. He did not deal in abstract theories, but in that which is essential to the development of character, that which will enlarge the capacity of human minds for knowing God and increasing their power to do good. He spoke of those truths that deal with the way people live, truths that will unite them with God.

Christ's teaching, like His sympathies, embraced the world. Never can there be a circumstance of life, a crisis in human experience, that has not been anticipated in His teaching, and for which its principles do not have a lesson. The Prince of teachers, His words will be found a guide to His co-workers till the end of time.

To Him the present and the future, the near and the far, were one. He had in view the needs of the whole world. Before His mind's eye was outspread every scene of human effort and achievement, of temptation and conflict, of perplexity and peril.

He spoke not only for, but to, the entire human family—to the little child, in the gladness of life's morning; to the eager, restless heart of youth; to men and women in the strength of their years, bearing the burden of responsibility and care; to the aged in their weakness and weariness. He spoke to every person in every land and in every age.

The things of this life He placed as subordinate to those of eternal interest, but He did not ignore their importance. He taught that heaven and earth are linked together, and that a knowledge of divine truth prepares people better to perform the duties of daily life. To Him nothing was without purpose. The sports of the child, the work of men and women, life's pleasures and cares and pains, all were means to one end—the revelation of God for the uplifting of humanity.

From His lips the Word of God came home to human hearts with new power and new meaning. In all the facts and experiences of life were revealed a divine lesson and the possibility of divine companionship. Again God dwelt on earth; human hearts became conscious of His presence; the world was encompassed with His love.

In the Teacher sent from God, all true educational work finds its center. Of this work today as verily as of the work He established during His earthly ministry the Savior speaks in the words: "I am the Alpha and the Omega, the Beginning and the End." Rev. 21:6.

In the presence of such a Teacher, of such opportunity for divine education, it is worse than folly to seek an education apart from Him. Behold, He is still inviting: "Let anyone who is thirsty come to Me, and let the one who believes in Me drink." John 7:37, 38, NRSV.

Chapter 9

An Illustration
of His Methods

The most complete illustration of Christ's methods as a teacher is found in His training of the first disciples. Upon these twelve men were to rest weighty responsibilities. He had chosen them as men whom He could imbue with His Spirit, and who could be fitted to carry forward His work on earth when He should leave it. To them, above all others, He gave the advantage of His own companionship. Through personal association He impressed Himself upon these chosen colaborers. "The life was manifested," says John the beloved, "and we have seen, and bear witness." 1 John 1:12.

Only by the communion of mind with mind and heart with heart, of the human with the divine, can be communicated that vitalizing energy which it is the work of true education to impart.

In the training of His disciples the Savior followed the system of education established at the beginning. The Twelve, with a few others who ministered to their needs and were from time to time connected with them, formed the family of Jesus. They accompanied Him on His journeys, shared His trials and hardships, and, as much as possible, entered into His work.

Sometimes He taught them as they sat together on the mountainside, sometimes beside the sea or from the fisherman's boat, sometimes as they walked together. Whenever He spoke to the multitude, the disciples formed the inner circle. They pressed close beside Him that they might lose nothing of His instruction. They were attentive listeners, eager to understand the truths they were to teach in all lands and to all ages.

The first pupils of Jesus were chosen from the ranks of the common people. They were humble, unlettered fishermen unschooled in the learning and customs of the rabbis, but trained by the stern discipline of toil and hardship. They had native ability and a teachable spirit. They could be instructed and molded for the Savior's work. In the common walks of life there are many workers patiently treading the round of their daily tasks, unconscious of latent powers that, if roused to action, would place them among the world's great leaders. Such were those who were called by the Savior to be His colaborers. And they had the advantage of three years' training by the greatest educator this world has ever known.

In these first disciples there was marked diversity. Destined to be the world's teachers, they represented widely varied types of character. There were Levi Matthew the publican, called from a life of business and subservience to Rome; Simon the zealot, an uncompromising foe of the imperial authority; warmhearted Peter, impulsive and self-sufficient, with Andrew his brother; Judas the Judean, polished, capable, and mean-spirited; Philip and Thomas, faithful and earnest yet slow of heart to believe; James the less and Jude, of less prominence among the group but men of force, positive both in their faults and in their virtues; Nathanael, a child in sincerity and trust; and the ambitious, loving-hearted sons of Zebedee.

In order to carry forward their work successfully, these disciples, differing widely in natural characteristics, in training, and in habits of life, needed to come into unity of feeling, thought, and action. To secure this unity, Christ worked to bring them into unity with Himself. The burden of His efforts for them is expressed in His prayer to the Father, "that they all may be one; as You, Father, are in Me, and I in You, that they also may be one in Us: . . . that the world may know that You have sent Me, and have loved them, as You have loved Me." John 17:21-23.

The Transforming Power of Christ

Of the twelve disciples, four were to act a leading part, each in a distinct way. In preparation for this, Christ taught them, foreseeing all: James, destined to swift death by the sword; John, who followed his Master the longest in labor and persecution; Peter, the pioneer in teaching the heathen world; and Judas, in service more capable than his associates, yet brooding in his soul—these were the objects of Christ's greatest solicitude and the ones who received His most frequent and careful instruction.

Peter, James, and John sought every opportunity to come into close contact with their Master, and their desire was granted. Of all the Twelve their relationship to Him was closest. John could be satisfied only with a still closer intimacy, and this he obtained. At that first conference beside the Jordan, when Andrew, having heard Jesus, hurried away to call his brother, John sat silent, rapt in the contemplation of wondrous themes. He followed the Savior, ever an eager, absorbed listener.

Yet John's character was not faultless. He and his brother were called "Sons of thunder." Mark 3:17. John was proud, ambitious, and combative, but beneath all this the divine Teacher discerned a sincere, loving heart. Jesus rebuked his self-seeking, disappointed his ambitions, and tested his faith, but He revealed to him that for which his soul longed—the beauty of holiness, His own transforming love. To His Father He said, "I have made Your name known to those whom You gave Me from the world." John 17:6, NRSV.

John's was a nature that longed for love, sympathy, and companionship. As a flower drinks in the sun and dew, so he drank in the divine light and life. In adoration and love he beheld the Savior, until his character reflected the character of his Master. "Behold," he said, "what manner of love the Father has bestowed on us, that we should be called children of God." 1 John 3:1.

From Weakness to Strength

The history of none of the disciples better illustrates Christ's method of training than does the history of Peter. Bold, aggressive, and self-confident, Peter often erred and often received reproof, yet his warmhearted loyalty and devotion to Christ were recognized and commended. Patiently and lovingly the Savior dealt with His impetuous disciple, seeking to check his self-confidence, and to teach him humility, obedience, and trust. But only in part was the lesson learned. Self-assurance was not uprooted.

Often Jesus attempted to open to the disciples the scenes of His trial and suffering, but the knowledge was unwelcome, and they did not see. Self-pity, which shrank from fellowship with Christ in suffering, prompted Peter's protest, "Far be it from You, Lord; this shall not happen to You!" Matt. 16:22. His words expressed the thought and feeling of the Twelve.

So they went on, the crisis drawing nearer. They were boastful and contentious, hoping for high positions, and not dreaming of the cross.

Peter's experience in betraying Jesus had a lesson for them all. To self-trust, trial is defeat. Christ could not prevent the sure outcome of unforsaken evil, but as His hand had been outstretched to save when the waves were about to sweep over Peter, so did His love reach out for his rescue when the deep waters swept over his soul. Again and again, on the very verge of ruin, Peter's words of boasting brought him nearer and still nearer to the brink. Over and over again was given the warning, "You will deny three times that you know Me." Luke 22:34. But the grieved, loving heart of the disciple responded, "Lord, I am ready to go with You, both to prison, and to death" (Luke 22:33). And He who reads the heart gave to Peter the message, little valued then, but that in the swift-falling darkness would shed a ray of hope: "Simon, Simon! Indeed, Satan has asked for you, that he may sift you as wheat. But I have prayed for you, that your faith should not fail: and when you have returned to Me, strengthen your brethren." Luke 22:31, 32.

When in the judgment hall the words of denial had been spoken; when Peter's love and loyalty, awakened under the Savior's glance of pity, love, and sorrow, had sent him forth to the garden where Christ had wept and prayed; when his tears of remorse dropped on the ground— then the Savior's words were an anchor for his soul. Christ, though foreseeing his sin, had not abandoned him to despair.

If the look that Jesus directed toward him had spoken condemnation instead of pity, how dense would have been the darkness that encompassed Peter, how reckless the despair of his tortured soul! In that hour of anguish and self-abhorrence, what could have held him back from the path trodden by Judas?

He who could not spare His disciple the anguish, did not leave him alone to its bitterness. His is a love that never fails nor forsakes.

Human beings, themselves given to evil, cannot read the heart; they do not know its struggle and pain. They need to learn of the rebuke that is love, of the blow that wounds to heal, of the warning that speaks hope.

It was not John, the one who watched with Jesus in the judgment hall, the one who stood beside His cross, and who of the Twelve was first at the tomb—it was not John, but Peter, who was mentioned by Christ after His resurrection. "Tell His disciples—and Peter," the angel said, "that He is going before you into Galilee; there you will see Him." Mark 16:7.

At the last meeting of Christ with the disciples by the sea, Peter, tested three times by the question, "Do you love Me?" was restored to his place among the Twelve. His work was appointed him; he was to feed the Lord's flock. Then, as His last personal direction, Jesus said, "You follow Me." John 21:17, 22. Now he could appreciate the words. Knowing more fully both his own weakness and Christ's power, he was ready to trust and obey. In His strength he could follow his Master.

At the close of his ministry, the disciple once so unready to discern the cross counted it a joy to yield up his life for the gospel, feeling only that to die in the same manner as his Master died was too great an honor.

Peter's transformation was a miracle of divine tenderness. It is a life lesson to all who desire to follow in the steps of the Master Teacher.

A Lesson in Love

Jesus warned, cautioned, and reproved His disciples, but neither John, Peter, nor the other disciples left Him. Notwithstanding the reproofs, they chose to be with Jesus. And the Savior did not, because of their errors, withdraw from them. If they will be disciplined and taught by Jesus, He takes men and women as they are, with all their faults and weaknesses, and trains them for His service.

But there was one of the Twelve to whom Christ spoke no word of direct reproof until very near the close of His work.

Judas introduced an element of antagonism among the disciples. In connecting with Jesus he had responded to the attraction of His character and life. He had sincerely desired a change in himself, and had hoped to experience this through being with Jesus. But this desire did not become predominant. He was ruled by the hope of selfish benefit in the worldly kingdom that he expected Christ to establish. Though recognizing the divine power of the love of Christ, Judas continued to cherish his own judgment, opinions, and his disposition to criticize and condemn. Christ's motives and movements, often so far above his comprehension, excited doubt and disapproval, and his own questionings and ambitions were insinuated to the disciples. Many of their contentions for supremacy, and much of their dissatisfaction with Christ's methods, originated with Judas.

Jesus, seeing that to antagonize was but to harden, refrained from direct conflict. Christ endeavored to heal the narrowing selfishness of Judas' life through contact with His own self-sacrificing love. In His teaching He unfolded principles that struck at the root of the disciple's self-centered ambitions. Lesson after lesson was thus given, and many a time Judas realized that his character had been portrayed and his sin pointed out, but he would not yield.

Mercy's pleading having been resisted, the impulse of evil bore final sway. Angered at an implied rebuke and made desperate by the disappointment of his ambitious dreams, Judas surrendered his soul to the demon of greed and determined to betray his Master. From the Passover chamber and the joy of Christ's presence he went forth to his evil work.

"Jesus knew from the beginning who they were who did not believe, and who would betray Him." John 6:64. Yet, knowing all, He had withheld no pleading of mercy or gift of love.

Seeing his danger, Christ had brought Judas close to Himself, within the inner circle of His chosen and trusted disciples. Day after day, when the burden lay heaviest upon His own heart, He had borne the pain of continual contact with that stubborn, suspicious, brooding spirit. He had witnessed and labored to counteract among His disciples that continuous, secret, subtle antagonism. And all this that no possible saving influence might be lacking to that imperiled soul!

So far as Judas himself was concerned, Christ's work of love had been to no avail. But to the other disciples it ever would be an example of tenderness and longsuffering as they dealt with the tempted and erring. And it had other lessons. At the ordination of the Twelve, the disciples had greatly desired that Judas should become one of their number. He had come more into contact with the world than they, he was a man of discernment and executive ability, and, having a high estimate of his own qualifications, he had led the disciples to hold him in the same regard. But the methods he wanted to introduce into Christ's work were based on principles aimed to achieve worldly recognition and honor. The working out of these desires in the life of Judas helped the disciples to understand the antagonism between the principle of self-aggrandizement and Christ's principle of humility and self-sacrifice. In the fate of Judas they saw the end to which self-serving tends.

For these disciples the mission of Christ finally accomplished its purpose. Little by little His example and lessons of self-denial molded their characters. His death destroyed their hope of worldly greatness. The fall of Peter, the apostasy of Judas, their own failure in forsaking Christ in

His anguish and peril, swept away their self-sufficiency. As they saw their own weakness and something of the greatness of the work committed to them, they felt their need of their Master's guidance at every step.

Many of His lessons, when spoken, they had not appreciated or understood; now they longed to recall these lessons, to hear again His words. With what joy His assurance now came back to them: "The Helper . . . whom the Father will send in My name, He will teach you all things, and bring to your remembrance all things that I said to you." John 14:26.

The disciples had seen Christ ascend from the Mount of Olives. And as the heavens received Him, there had come back to them His parting promise, "Lo, I am with you always, even to the end of the age." Matt. 28:20. They knew that His sympathies were still with them. They knew that they had a representative, an advocate, at the throne of God. In the name of Jesus they presented their petitions, repeating His promise, "Whatever you ask the Father in My name, He will give you." John 16:23.

Faithful to His promise, the Divine One, exalted in the heavenly courts, imparted of His fullness to His followers on earth. His enthronement at God's right hand was signaled by the outpouring of the Holy Spirit on His disciples. By the work of Christ these disciples had been led to feel their need of the Spirit, and under the Spirit's teaching they received their final preparation and went forth to their lifework.

No longer were they ignorant and uncultured. No longer were they a collection of independent units or discordant and conflicting elements. No longer were their hopes set on worldly greatness. They were of "one accord," of one mind and one soul. Christ filled their thoughts. The advancement of His kingdom was their aim. In mind and character they had become like their Master, and people "realized that they had been with Jesus." Acts 4:13.

Then there was such a revelation of the glory of Christ as never before had been witnessed by mortals. Through the cooperation of the divine Spirit the labors of the humble men whom Christ had chosen stirred the world. In a single generation the gospel was carried to every nation under heaven.

The presence of the same Spirit that instructed the disciples of old will produce the same results in educational work today. This is the end to which true education tends. This is the work that God designs it to accomplish.

C h a p t e r   10

God
in Nature

On all created things is seen the impress of the Deity. Nature testifies of God. The susceptible mind, brought into contact with the miracle and mystery of the universe, cannot but recognize the working of infinite power. Not by its own inherent energy does the earth produce its bounties and year by year continue its motion around the sun. An unseen hand guides the planets in their circuit of the heavens.

The same power that upholds nature is working also in humankind. The same great laws that guide both the star and the atom control human life. The laws that govern the heart's action, regulating the flow of the current of life to the body, are the laws of the mighty Intelligence that has jurisdiction of the soul. From Him all life proceeds. Its true sphere of action can be found only in harmony with Him. To transgress His law, physical, mental, or moral, is to place one's self out of harmony with the universe, introducing discord, anarchy, and ruin.

To those who learn thus to interpret its teachings, all nature becomes illuminated; the world is a lesson book, life a school. The unity of human beings with nature and with God, the universal dominion of law, the results of transgression, cannot fail to impress the mind and mold the character.

These are lessons that our children need to learn. To the little child nature presents an unfailing source of instruction and delight. And for those of older years, needing its silent reminders of the spiritual and eternal, nature's teaching will be no less a source of pleasure and instruction. The unseen is illustrated by the seen. On everything they may see the image and superscription of God.

So far as possible, children from their earliest years should be placed where this wonderful lesson book is open before them. Let them look at the glorious scenes painted by the great Master Artist on the shifting canvas of the heavens; let them become acquainted with the wonders of earth and sea; let them watch the unfolding mysteries of the changing seasons, and in all His works learn of the Creator.

Lay a True Foundation

In no other way can the foundation of a true education be so firmly and surely laid. Yet even children, as they come into contact with nature, cannot but recognize the working of antagonistic forces. It is here that nature needs an interpreter. Looking upon the evil manifest even in the natural world, all have the same sorrowful lesson to learn: "An enemy has done this." Matt. 13:28.

Only in the light that shines from Calvary can nature's teaching be read aright. Through the story of Bethlehem and the cross let it be shown how good is to conquer evil, and how every blessing that comes to us is a gift of redemption.

In brier and thorn, in thistle and tare, is represented the evil that blights and mars. In the singing bird and opening blossom, in ten thousand objects in nature, from the oak of the forest to the violet that blossoms at its root, is seen the love that restores. Nature still speaks to us of God's goodness.

"I know the thoughts that I think toward you, says the Lord, thoughts of peace and not of evil." Jer. 29:11. This is the message that, in the light from the cross, may be read on all the face of nature. The heavens declare His glory, and the earth is full of His riches.

Lessons of Life

The Great Teacher brought His hearers into contact with nature that they might listen to the voice which speaks in all created things. As their hearts became tender and their minds receptive, He helped them to interpret the spiritual teaching of the scenes on which their eyes rested. The parables, by means of which He loved to teach lessons of truth, show how open His spirit was to the influences of nature and how He delighted to gather the spiritual teaching from the surroundings of daily life.

The birds of the air, the lilies of the field, the sower and the seed, the shepherd and the sheep—with these Christ illustrated immortal truth. He drew illustrations also from the events of life, facts of experience familiar to His audience—the leaven, the hid treasure, the pearl, the fishing net, the lost coin, the prodigal son, the houses on the rock and the sand. In His lessons there was something to interest every mind and appeal to every heart. Thus the daily task, instead of being a mere round of toil, bereft of higher thoughts, was brightened and uplifted by constant reminders of the spiritual and the unseen.

So we should teach. Let children learn to see in nature an expression of the love and wisdom of God. Let the thought of Him be linked with bird and flower and tree. Let all things seen become interpreters of the unseen.

In this way all the events of life will be a means of divine teaching.

As they learn thus to study the lessons in all created things and in all life's experiences, show that the same laws are given for our good, and that only in obedience to them can we find true happiness and success.

The Law of Ministry

All things both in heaven and in earth declare that the great law of life is a law of service. The infinite Father ministers to the life of every living thing. Christ came to the earth "as the One who serves." Luke 22:27. The angels are "ministering spirits sent forth to minister for those who will inherit salvation." Heb. 1:14. The same law of service is written on all things in nature. The birds of the air, the beasts of the field, the trees of the forest, the leaves, the grass, and the flowers, the sun in the heavens, and the stars of light—all have their ministry. Lake and ocean, river and water spring—each takes to give.

As each thing in nature ministers to the world's life, it also secures its own. "Give, and it shall be given to you" (Luke 6:38) is the lesson written no less surely in nature than in the pages of God's Word.

As the hillsides and the plains open a channel for the mountain stream to reach the sea, that which they give is repaid a hundredfold. The stream that goes singing on its way leaves behind its gift of beauty and fruitfulness. Through the fields, bare and brown under the summer's heat, a line of green marks the river's course. Every noble tree, every bud, every blossom, is a witness of God's grace to all who become its channels to the world.

Sowing in Faith

Of the almost innumerable lessons taught in the varied processes of growth, some of the most precious are conveyed in the Savior's parable of the growing seed. It has lessons for both old and young.

"The kingdom of God is as if someone would scatter seed on the ground, and would sleep and rise night and day, and the seed would sprout and grow, he does not know how. The earth produces of itself; first the stalk, then the head, then the full grain in the head." Mark 4:26-28, NRSV.

The seed has a germinating principle, a principle that God Himself has implanted, yet if left to itself the seed would have no power to spring up. Human beings have their part to act in promoting the growth of the grain, but there is a point beyond which they can accomplish nothing. They must depend upon One who has connected the sowing and the reaping by wonderful links of His own omnipotent power.

There is life in the seed, there is power in the soil, but unless infinite power is exercised day and night, the seed will yield no return. The showers of rain must refresh the thirsty fields; the sun must impart warmth, electricity must be conveyed to the buried seed. The life that the Creator has implanted, He alone can call forth. Every seed grows, every plant develops, by the power of God.

The work of those who sow is a work of faith. They cannot understand the mystery of the germination and growth of the seed, but they have confidence in the agencies by which God causes vegetation to flourish. They scatter the seed, expecting to gather it manyfold in an abundant harvest. So parents and teachers are to work, expecting a harvest from the seed they sow.

For a time the good seed may lie unnoticed in the heart, giving no evidence that it has taken root. But afterward, as the Spirit of God breathes on the soul, the hidden seed springs up, and at last brings forth fruit. In our lifework we know not which shall prosper, this or that. This question is not for us to settle. God's great covenant declares that "while the earth remains, seedtime and harvest . . . shall not cease." Gen. 8:22. In the confidence of this promise, workers of the soil till and sow. Not less confidently are we, in the spiritual sowing, to work, trusting His assurance: "So shall My word be that goes forth from My mouth; it shall not return to Me void, but it shall accomplish what I please." Isa. 55:11.

The germination of the seed represents the beginning of spiritual life, and the development of the plant is a figure of the development of character. There can be no life without growth. The plant must either grow or die. As its growth is silent and imperceptible, but continuous, so is growth of character. At every stage of development our life may be perfect, yet if God's purpose for us is fulfilled, there will be constant advancement.

The plant grows by receiving that which God has provided to sustain its life. So spiritual growth is attained through cooperation with divine agencies. As the plant takes root in the soil, so we are to take root in Christ. As the plant receives sunshine, dew, and rain, so are we to receive the Holy Spirit. If our hearts are committed to Christ, as the Sun of Righteousness

He will arise upon us "with healing in His wings." Mal. 4:2. We shall "grow like the lily." Hosea 14:5.

Jesus Our Example

The gradual development of the plant from the seed is an object lesson in child training. There is "first the stalk, then the head, then the full grain in the head." Mark 4:28, NRSV. He who gave this parable created the tiny seed, gave it its vital properties, and ordained the laws that govern its growth. And the truths taught by the parable were made a reality in His own life. He, the Majesty of heaven, the King of glory, became a baby in Bethlehem, and for a time represented the helpless infant in its mother's care. In childhood He spoke and acted as a child, honoring His parents and carrying out their wishes in helpful ways. But from the first dawning of intelligence He was constantly growing in grace and in a knowledge of truth.

Parents and teachers should aim to cultivate the tendencies of the young so that at each stage of life they may represent the beauty appropriate to that period, unfolding naturally as do plants in the garden.

The little ones should be educated in childlike simplicity. They should be trained to be content with the small, helpful duties and pleasures and experiences natural to their years. Childhood answers to the stalk in the parable, and the stalk has a beauty peculiarly its own. Children should not be forced into a precocious maturity. As long as possible, they should retain the freshness and grace of their early years. The more quiet and simple their life—the more free from artificial excitement and the more in harmony with nature—the more favorable it is to physical and mental vigor and to spiritual strength.

In the Savior's miracle of feeding the five thousand is illustrated the working of God's power in the production of the harvest. In multiplying the seed cast into the ground, He who multiplied the loaves is working a miracle every day. By a miracle He constantly feeds millions of people from earth's harvest fields. Human beings are called upon to cooperate with Him in the care of the grain and the preparation of the loaf, and because of this they lose sight of the divine agency. The working of His power is ascribed to natural causes or to human instrumentality. Too often His gifts are perverted to selfish uses and made a curse instead of a blessing. God is seeking to change all this. He desires that our dull senses shall be quickened to discern His merciful kindness, that His gifts may be to us the blessing that He intended.

It is the word of God, the impartation of His life, that gives life to the seed, and we, in eating the grain, become partakers of that life. God desires that even in receiving our daily bread we may recognize His agency and be brought into closer fellowship with Him.

By the laws of God in nature, effect follows cause with unvarying certainty. The reaping testifies to the sowing. Here no pretense is tolerated. Mortals may deceive other mortals and may receive praise and compensation for service they have not rendered. But in nature there can be no deception. On the unfaithful husbandman the harvest passes sentence of condemnation.

And in the highest sense this is true also in the spiritual realm. It is in appearance, not in reality, that evil succeeds. People in any business or profession who are untrue to their highest responsibilities may flatter themselves that so long as the wrong is concealed they are gaining an advantage. But not so; they are cheating themselves. The harvest of life is character, and it is this that determines destiny, both for this life and for the life to come.

The harvest is a reproduction of the seed sown. Every seed yields fruit after its kind. So it is with the traits of character we cherish. Selfishness, self-love, self-esteem, self-indulgence, reproduce themselves, and the end is wretchedness and ruin. If you "sow to your own flesh, you will reap corruption from the flesh; but if you sow to the Spirit, you will reap eternal life from the Spirit." Gal. 6:8, NRSV. Love, sympathy, and kindness yield the fruit of blessing, a harvest that is imperishable.

In the harvest the seed is multiplied. A single grain of wheat, increased by repeated sowings, would cover a whole land with golden sheaves. The influence of a single life, of even a single act, may be just as widespread.

What deeds of love the memory of that alabaster box broken for Christ's anointing has prompted through the long centuries! What countless gifts that contribution of "two mites" by a poor unnamed widow has brought to the Savior's cause!

Life Through Death
The lesson of seed sowing teaches liberality. "The one who sows spar-

ingly will also reap sparingly, and the one who sows bountifully will also reap bountifully." 2 Cor. 9:6, NRSV.

The Lord says, "Blessed are you who sow beside all waters." Isa. 32:20. To sow beside all waters means to give wherever help is needed. This will not tend to poverty. By casting it away the sower multiplies the seed. So it is that by imparting we increase our blessings. God's promise assures a sufficiency, that we may continue to give.

By the casting of grain into the earth the Savior represents His sacrifice for us. "Unless a grain of wheat falls into the ground and dies," He says, "it remains alone; but if it dies, it produces much grain." John 12:24. Only through the sacrifice of Christ, the Seed, could fruit be brought forth for the kingdom of God.

So it is with all who bring forth fruit as workers together with Christ. Self-love, self-interest, must perish. The life must be cast into the furrow of the world's need. But the law of self-sacrifice is the law of self-preservation. The husbandman preserves his grain by casting it away. So the life that will be preserved is the life that is freely given in service to God and humanity.

Prepare the Heart for the Seed of Truth

As parents and teachers try to teach these lessons, the work should be made practical. Children should themselves prepare the soil and sow the seed. As they work, parents and teachers can explain the garden of the heart, with the good or bad seed sown there. They can explain that as the garden must be prepared for the natural seed, so the heart must be prepared for the seed of truth. As the seed is sown in the ground, they can teach the lesson of Christ's death, and the truth of the resurrection as the blade springs up. As the plant grows, the comparisons between the natural and the spiritual sowing may be continued.

Young people should be instructed in a similar way. From the tilling of the soil, lessons may constantly be learned. No one settles on a raw piece of land with the expectation that it will yield a harvest at once. Diligent, persevering work must be put forth to prepare the ground, sow the seed, and cultivate the crop. So it must be in the spiritual sowing. The garden of the heart must be cultivated. The soil of the heart must be broken up by repentance. Evil growth that chokes good grain must be uprooted. As land once overgrown by thorns can be reclaimed only by diligent work, so the evil tendencies of the heart can be overcome only by earnest effort in the name and strength of Christ.

In the cultivation of the soil the thoughtful workers will find that treasures little dreamed of open up before them. No one can succeed in agriculture or gardening without attention to the laws involved. The special needs of every variety of plant must be studied. Different varieties require different soil and cultivation, and conformity to the laws regulating each is the condition of success.

The attention required in transplanting—so that not even a root fiber is crowded or misplaced—the care of the young plants, pruning and watering, weeding and controlling pests, not only teach important lessons concerning the development of character, but the work itself is a means of development. Cultivating carefulness, patience, attention to detail, and obedience to law, imparts a most essential training. The constant contact with the mystery of life and the loveliness of nature, as well as the tenderness called forth in ministering to these beautiful objects of God's creation, tends to quicken the mind and refine and elevate the character. The lessons taught prepare the worker to deal more successfully with other minds.

Other Object Lessons

God's healing power runs all through nature. If a tree is cut, if a human being is wounded or breaks a bone, nature begins at once to repair the injury. Even before the need exists, the healing agencies are ready, and as soon as a part is wounded, every energy focuses on the work of restoration.

So it is in the spiritual realm. Before sin created the need, God provided the remedy. Every soul who yields to temptation is wounded by the adversary, but whenever there is sin, there is the Savior. It is Christ's work "to heal the brokenhearted, to preach deliverance to the captives, . . . to set at liberty those who are oppressed." Luke 4:18.

In this work we are to cooperate. "If anyone is detected in a transgression . . . restore such a one." Gal. 6:1, NRSV. The word here translated "restore" means to put in joint, as a dislocated bone. How appropriate the figure! People who fall into error or sin are thrown out of relation to everything about them. They may realize their error and be filled with remorse, but they cannot recover themselves. They are confused and perplexed. They are to be reclaimed, healed, re-established. "You who have received the Spirit should restore" them. Only the love that flows from the heart of Christ can heal. Only a person in whom that love flows, even as the sap in the tree or the blood in the body, can restore the wounded soul.

Love's agencies have wonderful power, for they are divine. The soft answer that "turns away wrath," the love that "suffers long and is kind," the charity that "will cover a multitude of sins" (Prov. 15:1; 1 Cor.13:4; 1 Peter 4:8)—if we would learn the lesson, our lives would be gifted with power for healing. Life would be transformed, and the earth would become a likeness and foretaste of heaven!

All Can Understand Nature's Lessons

These precious lessons may be taught so simply as to be understood even by little children. The heart of the child is tender and easily impressed, and when we who are older become "as little children" (Matt. 18:3), when we learn the simplicity, gentleness, and tender love of the Savior, we shall not find it difficult to touch the hearts of the little ones and teach them love's ministry of healing.

Perfection exists in the least as well as in the greatest works of God. The hand that hung the worlds in space is the hand that fashions the flowers of the field. Examine under the microscope the smallest and most common of wayside blossoms, and note the exquisite beauty and completeness in all its parts. The most common tasks, performed with loving faithfulness, are beautiful in God's sight. Conscientious attention to little things will make us workers together with Him and win His commendation.

As the bow in the cloud results from the union of sunshine and shower, so the bow above God's throne represents the union of His mercy and His justice. To the sinful but repentant soul God says, Live, for "I have found a ransom." Job 33:24. "The mountains shall depart and the hills be removed, but My kindness shall not depart from you, nor shall My covenant of peace be removed, says the Lord who has mercy on you." Isa. 54:10.

The Message of the Stars and Nature

The stars also have a message of good cheer for every human being. In those hours that come to all, when obstacles seem insurmountable and life's aims impossible to achieve, courage and steadfastness can be found in that lesson which God counsels us to learn from the stars in their untroubled course. "Lift up your eyes on high, and see who has created these things, who brings out their host by number; He calls them all by name, by the greatness of His might and the strength of His power; not one is missing." Isa. 40:26.

The palm tree, beaten by the scorching sun and the fierce sandstorm, stands green and fruitful in the midst of the desert. Its roots are fed by living springs. Its crown of green is seen afar over the parched, desolate plain, and the traveler, ready to die, urges his failing steps to the cool shade and life-giving water.

The tree of the desert is a symbol of what God means the life of His children to be. They are to guide weary souls, ready to perish in the desert of sin, to the living water. They are to point lost men and women to Him who gives the invitation, "If anyone thirsts, let him come to Me, and drink." John 7:37.

A wide, deep river that serves as a highway for the traffic of nations, is valued as a worldwide benefit. But what of the little rills that help to form this giant stream? Without them, the river would disappear. Upon them its very existence depends. So men and women who are called to lead in some great work are honored as if its success were due to them alone. But that success required the faithful cooperation of humble workers almost without number—people of whom the world knows nothing. Service without recognition is the lot of most of the world's workers. Many are filled with discontent and feel that life is wasted. But the little rill that makes its noiseless way through grove and meadow is as useful in its way as the broad river. And in contributing to the river's life, it helps achieve that which it could never accomplish alone.

This lesson is needed by many. Talent is too much idolized, and station too much coveted. Many people will do nothing unless they are recognized as leaders. Too many must receive praise or they have no interest in the work. We need to learn faithfulness in making the utmost use of the powers and opportunities we have, and contentment in the lot to which Heaven assigns us.

A Lesson of Trust

"Now ask the beasts, and they will teach you; and the birds of the air, and they will tell you: . . . and the fish of the sea will explain to you." "Go to the ant; . . . consider her ways." Job 12:7, 8; Prov. 6:6.

We are not merely to tell our children about these creatures of God, the animals themselves are to be their teachers. Ants teach lessons of patient industry, of perseverance in surmounting obstacles, of providence for the future. Birds teach the lesson of trust. Our heavenly Father provides for them, but they must gather food, build nests, and rear their young. Every moment enemies seek to destroy them, yet they go about their work cheerily! Their little songs are full of joy!

God sends springs of water to run among the hills where the birds live and "sing among the branches." Ps. 104:12. All the creatures of the woods and hills are part of His great household. He opens His hand and satisfies "the desire of every living thing." Ps. 145:16.

The eagle of the Alps is sometimes beaten down by the tempest into the narrow defiles of the mountains. Storm clouds shut in this mighty bird of the forest, their dark masses separating her from the sunny heights where she has made her home. Her efforts to escape seem fruitless. She dashes to and fro, beating the air with her strong wings and waking the mountain echoes with her cries. At length, with a note of triumph, she darts upward, and, piercing the clouds, is once more in the clear sunlight, with the darkness and tempest far beneath.

So we may be surrounded with difficulties, discouragement, and darkness. Falsehood, calamity, injustice, shut us in. There are clouds that we cannot dispel. In vain we battle with circumstances. There is but one way of escape. Beyond the clouds God's light is shining. Into the sunlight of His presence we may rise on the wings of faith.

Many are the lessons that may be drawn from nature: for example, self-reliance, from the tree that, growing alone on plain or mountainside, strikes down its roots deep into the earth, and in its rugged strength defies the tempest; the power of early influence, from the gnarled, shapeless trunk, bent as a sapling, to which no earthly power can afterward restore its lost symmetry; the secret of a holy life, from the water lily, that, on the bosom of some slimy pool, surrounded by weeds and rubbish, strikes down its channeled stem to the pure sands beneath, and, drawing thence its life, displays its fragrant blossoms in spotless purity.

Thus while the children and youth gain a knowledge of facts from teachers and textbooks, let them learn to draw lessons and discern truth for themselves. In their gardening, question them as to what they learn from the care of their plants. As they look on a beautiful landscape, ask them why God clothed the fields and woods with such lovely and varied hues. Why was not all a somber brown? When they gather flowers, lead them to think why He saved for us the beauty of these wanderers from Eden. Teach them to notice the evidences in nature of God's thought for us, the wonderful adaptation of all things to our need and happiness.

Many illustrations from nature are used by the Bible writers, and as we observe the things of the natural world, we shall be enabled, under the guidance of the Holy Spirit, to understand more fully the lessons of God's Word. It is thus that nature becomes a key to the treasure house of the Word.

Children should be encouraged to search out in nature the objects that illustrate Bible teachings, and to trace in the Bible the lessons drawn from nature. In this way they may learn to see Him in tree and vine, in lily and rose, in sun and star. They may learn to hear His voice in the song of birds, in the sighing of the trees, in the rolling thunder, and in the music of the sea. Every object in nature will repeat to them His precious lessons.

To those who thus acquaint themselves with Christ, the earth will never again be a lonely and desolate place. It will be their Father's house, filled with the presence of Him who once walked on earth.

C h a p t e r   13

Mental and Spiritual Culture

For the mind and the soul, as well as for the body, it is God's law that strength is acquired by effort. In harmony with this law, God has provided in His Word the means for mental and spiritual development.

The Bible contains all the principles that human beings need to understand in order to be fitted both for this life and for the life to come. And these principles may be understood by all. No one with a spirit to appreciate its teaching can read a single passage from the Bible without gaining some helpful thought. But the most valuable teaching of the Bible is not obtained by occasional or disconnected study. Its great system of truth cannot be discerned by the hasty or careless reader. Many of its treasures lie far beneath the surface, and can be obtained only by diligent research and continuous effort.

The truths that go to make up the great whole must be searched out and gathered up, "here a little, there a little." Isa. 28:10. When thus searched out and brought together, they will be found to be perfectly fitted to one another. Each Gospel is a supplement to the others, every prophecy an explanation of another, every truth a development of some other truth. Every principle in the Word of God has its place, every fact its bearing. And the complete structure, in design and execution, bears testimony to its

Author. Only the mind of the Infinite could conceive or fashion such a structure.

In searching out the various parts and studying their relationship, the highest faculties of the human mind are called into intense activity. No one can engage in such study without developing mental power.

Value of Bible Study

The mental value of Bible study consists not only in searching out truth and bringing it together, it consists also in the effort required to grasp the themes presented. The mind that is occupied only with commonplace matters becomes dwarfed and enfeebled. If never tasked to comprehend grand and far-reaching truths, it loses the power of growth. As a safeguard against this degeneracy and a stimulus to development, nothing can equal the study of God's Word. As a means of intellectual training, the Bible is more effective than any other book or all other books combined. No other study can impart such mental power as does the effort to grasp the stupendous truths of revelation. The mind thus brought into contact with the thoughts of the Infinite will expand and strengthen.

And even greater is the power of the Bible in the development of the spiritual nature. Human beings were created for fellowship with God, and only in such fellowship can they find real life and development. Men and women who with sincere and teachable spirits study God's Word, seeking to comprehend its truths, will be brought in touch with its Author. Except by their own choice, there is no limit to the possibilities of their development.

In its wide range of style and subjects the Bible has something to interest every mind and appeal to every heart. In its pages are found history, biography, and principles of government for the state and for regulating the home—principles that human wisdom has never equaled. It contains the most profound philosophy and the sweetest, most sublime poetry. Immeasurably superior in value to the productions of any human author are the Bible writings even when thus considered; but of infinitely wider scope, of infinitely greater value, are they when viewed in their relation to the grand central thought. Viewed in the light of this thought, every topic has a new significance. In the most simply stated truths are involved principles that are as high as heaven and that compass eternity.

Theme of Redemption

The central theme of the Bible, the theme about which every other clusters, is the redemption plan, the restoration in the human soul of the image of God. From the first intimation of hope in the sentence pronounced in Eden to that last glorious promise of the Revelation— "They shall see His face; and His name shall be on their foreheads" (Rev. 22:4)—the burden of every book and every passage of the Bible is the unfolding of this wondrous theme—uplifting humanity—the power of God "who gives us the victory through our Lord Jesus Christ." 1 Cor. 15:57.

People who grasp this thought have before them an infinite field for study. They have the key that will unlock to them the whole treasure house of God's Word.

The science of redemption is the science of all sciences, the science that is the study of angels and all the intelligences of the unfallen worlds. It is the science that engages the attention of our Lord and Savior, the science that will be the study of God's redeemed throughout endless ages. This is the highest study in which it is possible for mortals to engage. It will quicken the mind and uplift the soul as no other study can.

The creative energy that called the worlds into existence is in the Word of God. This word imparts power; it begets life. Every command is a promise; accepted by the will and received into the soul, it brings with it the life of the Infinite One. It transforms the nature and recreates the soul in the image of God.

Feed Upon the Word

The mind, the soul, is built up by that on which it feeds, and it rests with us to determine what it shall be fed. It is within the power of everyone to choose the topics that shall occupy the thoughts and shape the character. Of every human being privileged with access to the Scriptures, God says, "Call to Me, and I will answer you, and show you great and mighty things, which you do not know." Jer. 33:3.

With the Word of God in their hands, human beings may have such companionship as they choose. In its pages they may interface with the best and most noble of the human race, and may listen to the voice of the Eternal. As they study and meditate on the themes into which "the angels desire to look" (1 Peter 1:12), they may have angel companionship. They may follow the steps of the heavenly Teacher, and listen to His words as He taught on mountain and plain and sea. Living as in the atmosphere of heaven, they may impart hope to others and longings for holiness. They may themselves come closer and still closer into fellowship with the Unseen, drawing nearer and nearer the threshold of the eternal world, until the portals shall open and they enter there. The voices that will greet them are the voices of the holy ones, who, unseen, were on earth their companions— voices that here they learned to distinguish and to love. Those who through the Word of God have lived in fellowship with heaven, will find themselves at home in heaven's companionship.

Chapter 14

Science
and the Bible

Since the book of nature and the book of revelation bear the impress of the same master mind, they cannot but speak in harmony. By different methods and in different languages they witness to the same great truths. Science is ever discovering new wonders, but from its research it brings nothing that, rightly understood, conflicts with divine revelation. The book of nature and the written Word shed light on each other. They make us acquainted with God by teaching us something of the laws through which He works.

But inferences erroneously drawn from facts observed in nature have led to supposed conflict between science and revelation. In the effort to restore harmony, interpretations of Scripture have been adopted that undermine and destroy the force of the Word of God. Geology has been thought to contradict the literal interpretation of the Mosaic record of the Creation. Millions of years, it is claimed, were required for the earth to evolve from chaos. In order to accommodate the Bible to this supposed revelation of science, the days of creation are assumed to have been vast, indefinite periods, covering thousands or even millions of years.

Such a conclusion is uncalled for. The Bible record is in harmony with itself and with the teaching of nature. Of the first day of Creation the record says, "The evening and the morning were the first day." Gen. 1:5. And the same, in substance, is said of each of the first six days of Creation week. Inspiration declares each of these periods to have been a day consisting of evening and morning, like every day since that time. In regard to the work of creation itself, the divine testimony is, "He spoke, and it was done; He commanded, and it stood fast." Ps. 33:9. With Him who could thus call into existence unnumbered worlds, how long a time would be required for the earth to evolve from chaos? In order to account for His works, must we do violence to His Word?

It is true that remains found in the earth testify to the existence of humans, animals, and plants much larger than any now known. These are regarded as proof that vegetable and animal life existed prior to the time of the Mosaic record. But Bible history furnishes ample explanation concerning these things. Before the Flood the development of vegetable and animal life was immeasurably superior to that which has since been known. At the Flood the surface of the earth was broken up, marked changes took place, and in the re-formation of the earth's crust many evidences of the life previously existing were preserved. The vast forests buried in the earth at the time of the Flood, and since changed to coal, form the extensive coal fields, and yield the supplies of oil that minister to our comfort and convenience. These things, as they are brought to light, are witnesses that mutely testify to the truth of the Word of God.

Revelations of Science

Like the theory concerning the evolution of the earth is the one that attributes to an ascending line of germs, mollusks, and quadrupeds the evolution of human beings, the crowning glory of the creation. In the light of the brevity of human life, the restricted vision of scientists, the frequent and great errors in their conclusions, the frequency with which their deductions are revised or cast aside, and how the theories of different scientists conflict with one another, shall we, for the privilege of tracing our descent from germs, mollusks, and apes, consent to do away with that inspired statement, so grand in its simplicity, "God created humankind in His image; in the image of God He created them"? Gen. 1:27, NRSV. Shall we reject that genealogical record—more treasured than any in the courts of kings—"which was the son of Adam, which was the son of God"? Luke 3:38, KJV.

Rightly understood, both the revelations of science and the experiences of life are in harmony with the testimony of Scripture to the constant working of God in nature.

In the hymn recorded by Nehemiah, the Levites sang, "You alone are the Lord; You have made heaven, the heaven of heavens, with all their host, the earth and everything in it, the seas, and all that is in them, and You preserve them all." Neh. 9:6.

Creation Has Been Completed

So far as this earth is concerned, Scripture declares the work of creation to have been completed. "The works were finished from the foundation of the world." Heb. 4:3. But the power of God is still exercised in upholding the objects of His creation. It is not by its own inherent energy that the heart beats, and breath follows breath. Every breath, every pulsation of the heart, is an evidence of the care of Him in whom we live and move and have our being. From the smallest insect to human beings, every living creature is daily dependent upon God's providence.

"These all wait for You. . . .
What you give them they gather:
You open Your hand, they are filled with good.
You hide your face, they are troubled;
You take away their breath, they die,
And return to their dust.
You send forth Your Spirit, they are created;
And You renew the face of the earth." Ps. 104:27-30.
See also Job 26:7-10; 26:11-14; Nahum 1:3.

The mighty power that works through all nature and sustains all things is not, as some scientists claim, merely an all-pervading principle, an actuating energy. God is a spirit, yet He is a personal being, for our first parents were made in His image. As a personal being, God has revealed Himself in His Son. Jesus, the outshining of the Father's glory "and the express image of His person" (Heb. 1:3), appeared on earth as a man. As a personal Savior He came to the world. As a personal Savior He ascended on high. As a personal Savior He intercedes in the heavenly courts. Dan. 7:13.

The apostle Paul, writing by the Holy Spirit, declares of Christ that "By Him all things were created that are in heaven and that are on earth.

... He is before all things, and in Him all things consist." Col. 1:16, 17. The hand that sustains the worlds in space, the hand that holds in their orderly arrangement and tireless activity all things throughout the universe of God, is the hand that was nailed to the cross.

The greatness of God is incomprehensible to us. "The Lord's throne is in heaven" (Ps. 11:4), yet by His Spirit He is present everywhere. He has an intimate knowledge of, and a personal interest in, all the works of His hand.

"You know my sitting down and my rising up,
You understand my thought afar off.
You comprehend my path and my lying down,
And are acquainted with all my ways.
Such knowledge is too wonderful for me.
It is high, I cannot attain it." Ps. 139:2, 3, 6.
See also Job 26:6; Ps. 113:5, 6; 139:7-10.

The Maker of all things ordained the wonderful adaptation of means to end, of supply to need. In the material world He provided that every desire implanted should be met. He created the human soul, with its capacity for knowing and for loving. And He has provided that the demands of the soul shall be satisfied. No intangible principle, no impersonal essence or mere abstraction, can satisfy the needs and longings of human beings in this life of struggle with sin and sorrow and pain. It is not enough to believe in law and force, in things that have no pity and never hear the cry for help. We need to know of an almighty arm that will hold us up, of an infinite Friend that pities us. We need to clasp a hand that is warm, to trust in a heart full of tenderness. And this is the way God has revealed Himself in His Word.

Science Recognizes God's Power

Human beings who study most deeply into the mysteries of nature will realize most fully their own ignorance and weakness. They will realize that there are depths and heights that they cannot reach, secrets they cannot penetrate. They will be ready to say, with Newton, "I seem to myself to have been like a child on the seashore finding pebbles and shells, while the great ocean of truth lay undiscovered before me."

The deepest students of science are compelled to recognize in nature the working of infinite power. But to unaided human reason, nature's teaching is contradictory and disappointing. Only in the light of revelation can it be read aright. "By faith we understand." Heb. 11:3.

"In the beginning God." Gen. 1:1. Here alone can the mind in its eager questioning find rest. Above, beneath, beyond, abides Infinite Love, working out all things to accomplish "the good pleasure of His goodness." 2 Thess. 1:11.

"For since the creation of the world His invisible attributes are clearly seen, being understood by the things that are made, even His eternal power and Godhead." Rom. 1:20. But their testimony can be understood only through the aid of the divine Teacher.

"When He, the Spirit of truth, has come, He will guide you into all truth." John 16:13. Only by the aid of that Spirit and the Word can the testimony of science be rightly interpreted. Only under the direction of the Omniscient One shall we, in the study of His works, be enabled to think His thoughts after Him.

Chapter 15

Business Principles and Methods

There is no branch of legitimate business for which the Bible does not afford an essential preparation. Its principles of diligence, honesty, thrift, temperance, and purity are the secret of true success. These principles, as set forth in the book of Proverbs, constitute a treasury of practical wisdom. Where can merchants, artisans, or directors of men and women in any department of business, find better maxims for themselves or for their employees than are found in these words of the wise man:

"Do you see those who are skillful in their work? they will serve kings; they will not serve common people." Prov. 22:29, NRSV. "The drunkard and the glutton will come to poverty, and drowsiness will clothe them with rags." Prov. 23:21, NRSV. "Whoever walks with the wise becomes wise." Prov. 13:20, NRSV.

The whole circle of our obligation to one another is covered by that counsel of Christ, "In everything do to others as you would have them do to you." Matt. 7:12, NRSV.

How many might have escaped financial failure and ruin by heeding the warnings so often repeated and emphasized in the Scriptures: "One who is in a hurry to be rich will not go unpunished." Prov. 28:20, NRSV. "Getting treasures by a lying tongue is the fleeting fancy of those who seek death." Prov. 21:6. "The borrower is servant to the lender." Prov. 22:7. "To guarantee loans for a stranger brings trouble, but there is safety in refusing to do so." Prov. 11:15, NRSV.

With these principles are bound up the well-being of society, of both secular and religious associations. They give security to property and life. For all that makes confidence and cooperation possible, the world is indebted to the law of God as given in His Word and as still traced in lines often obscure and well-nigh obliterated in human hearts. The psalmist's words, "The law of Your mouth is better to me than thousands of shekels of gold and silver" (Ps. 119:72), state an absolute truth and one that is recognized in the business world. Even in this age of passion for getting money, when competition is sharp and methods often are unscrupulous, it is still widely acknowledged that, for a young person starting in life, integrity, diligence, temperance, purity, and thrift constitute better capital than any amount of mere money.

Yet even of those who appreciate the value of these qualities and acknowledge the Bible as their source, but few recognize the principle on which they depend. That which lies at the foundation of business integrity and true success is recognition of God's ownership. As the Creator of all things, He is the original proprietor. We are His stewards. All that we have is a trust from Him, to be used according to His direction.

This obligation rests on every human being. It has to do with the whole sphere of human activity. Whether we recognize it or not, we are stewards, supplied by God with talents and faculties, and placed in the world to do a work appointed by Him.

To every person is given the work for which his or her capabilities are best suited, the work that will result in greatest good to the human race and bring greatest honor to God.

Thus our business or calling is a part of God's great plan, and so long as it is conducted in accordance with His will He is responsible for the results. As "God's servants, working together" (1 Cor. 3:9, NRSV), our part is faithful compliance with His directions. Thus there is no place for anxious care. Every faculty is to be exercised to its highest capacity, but the dependence will be, not on the successful outcome of our efforts, but on the promise of God. The word that fed Israel in the desert and sustained Elijah through the time of famine, has the same power today. "Therefore do not worry, saying 'What shall we eat?' or, 'What shall we drink?' . . .

Seek first the kingdom of God, and His righteousness, and all these things shall be added to you." Matt. 6:31-33.

The Tithe Is the Lord's

The God who gives human beings power to get wealth has with the gift bound up an obligation. Of all that we acquire He claims a specified portion. The tithe is the Lord's. "All the tithe of the land, whether of the seed of the land or of the fruit of the tree . . . the tithe of the herd or the flock, . . . shall be holy to the Lord." Lev. 27:30, 32.

"Bring all the tithes into the storehouse" (Mal. 3:10) is God's command. No appeal is made to gratitude or to generosity. This is a matter of simple honesty. The tithe is the Lord's, and He tells us to return to Him that which is His own.

"It is required in stewards, that they be found trustworthy." 1 Cor. 4:2, NRSV. If honesty is an essential principle of business life, must we not recognize our obligation to God—the obligation that underlies every other?

By the terms of our stewardship we are placed under obligation not only to God but to humanity. To the infinite love of the Redeemer every human being is indebted for the gifts of life. Food, clothing, and shelter; body, mind, and soul—all are the purchase of His blood. And by the obligation of gratitude and service thus imposed, Christ has bound us to all members of the human family. He bids us, "Through love serve one another." Gal. 5:13; see also Matt. 25:40; Rev. 1:14. By all that has blessed our life above others, we are placed under obligation to every human being whom we might benefit.

Never can we safely lose sight of the fact that the goods we handle are not our own. We are but stewards, and on the discharge of our obligation to God and needy humans depend both the welfare of other people and our own destiny for this life and for the life to come. "Cast your bread upon the water, for you will find it after many days." Eccl.11:1.

"Give, and it will be given to you: good measure, pressed down, shaken together, and running over will be put into your bosom. For with the same measure that you use, it will be measured back to you." Luke 6:38.

"Bring all the tithes into the storehouse, that there may be food in My house, and prove Me now in this," says the Lord of hosts, "if I will not open for you the windows of heaven and pour out for you such a blessing that there shall not be room enough to receive it. And I will rebuke the devourer for your sakes, so that he will not destroy the fruit of your ground, nor shall the vine fail to bear fruit for you in the field." Mal. 3:10, 11.

"Seek justice, rebuke the oppressor; defend the fatherless, plead for the widow." Isa. 1:17. "Whoever is kind to the poor lends to the Lord, and will be repaid in full." Prov. 19:17, NRSV. All who make this investment lay up double treasure. Besides that which, however wisely improved, they must leave at last, they are amassing wealth for eternity—that treasure of character that is the most valuable possession of earth or heaven.

Honest Business Dealings

"The Lord knows the days of the upright, and their inheritance shall be forever. They shall not be ashamed in the evil time, and in the days of famine they shall be satisfied." Ps. 37:18, 19.

God has given in His Word a picture of Job, a prosperous man—one whose life was in the truest sense a success, a person whom both heaven and earth delighted to honor. Of his experiences Job himself says:

"Just as I was in the days of my prime,
When the friendly counsel of God was over my tent;
When the Almighty was yet with me,
When my children were around me; . . .
When I went out to the gate by the city,
When I took my seat in the open square,
The young men saw me and hid,
And the aged arose and stood;
The princes refrained from talking,
And put their hand on their mouth;
The voice of the nobles was hushed." Job 29:4, 5; 7-10.
See also Job 31:32; 29:21-25.

"The blessing of the Lord makes one rich, and He adds no sorrow with it." Prov. 10:22.

The Bible shows also the result of a departure from right principles in our dealing both with God and with one another. To those who are entrusted with His gifts but indifferent to His claims, God says: "Consider how you have fared. You have sown much, and harvested little: you eat, but you never have enough; you drink, but you never have your fill; you clothe yourselves, but no one is warm; and you that earn wages, earn wages to put them into a bag with holes." Hag. 1:5, 6, NRSV.

"Will anyone rob God? Yet you are robbing Me! But you say, 'How are we robbing You?' In your tithes and offerings!" Mal. 3:8.

The accounts of every business, the details of every transaction, pass the scrutiny of unseen auditors, agents of Him who never compromises with injustice, never overlooks evil, never palliates wrong. "There is no darkness nor shadow of death where the workers of iniquity may hide themselves." Job 34:22.

Against all evildoers God's law utters condemnation. They may disregard that voice, they may seek to drown its warning, but in vain. It follows them, and makes itself heard. It destroys their peace. If unheeded, it pursues them to the grave. It bears witness against them at the judgment. A quenchless fire, it finally consumes soul and body.

"What will it profit them to gain the whole world and forfeit their life? Indeed, what can they give in return for their life?" Mark 8:36, 37, NRSV.

This is a question that demands consideration by every parent, every teacher, every student—by every human being, young or old. No scheme of business or plan of life can be sound or complete that embraces only the brief years of this present life and makes no provision for the unending future. Let the young be taught to take eternity into their reckoning. Teach them to choose the principles and seek the possessions that are enduring—to lay up for themselves that "treasure in the heavens that does not fail, where no thief approaches nor moth destroys." Luke 12:33.

All who do this are making the best possible preparation for life in this world. All who lay up treasure in heaven will find their life on earth enriched and ennobled.

"Godliness is profitable for all things, having promise of the life that now is and of that which is to come." 1 Tim. 4:8.

Chapter 16

Bible Biographies

No part of the Bible is of greater value as an educator than its biographies. These biographies differ from all others in that they are absolutely true to life. Only He who reads the heart, who discerns the secret springs of motive and action, can with absolute truth delineate character or give a faithful picture of a human life. In God's Word alone is found such delineation.

The Bible clearly teaches that what we do is the result of what we are. To a great degree the experiences of life are the fruit of our own thoughts and deeds. "A curse without cause shall not alight." Prov. 26:2. "Hear, O earth! Behold, I will certainly bring calamity on this people, even the fruit of their thoughts." Jer. 6:19.

Terrible is this truth, and deeply should it be impressed. Every deed reacts upon the doer. Human beings may recognize in the evils that curse their lives the fruitage of their own sowing. Nevertheless, we are not without hope.

Jacob Was Transformed

To gain the birthright that was already his by God's promise, Jacob resorted to fraud, and he reaped the harvest in the hatred of Esau, his brother.

Through twenty years of exile he was himself wronged and defrauded, and at last was forced to find safety in flight. And he reaped a second harvest as the evils of his own character were seen to crop out in his sons—all too true a picture of the retributions of human life.

But God says, "I will not contend forever, nor will I always be angry; for the spirit would fail before Me, and the souls which I have made. For the iniquity of his covetousness I was angry and struck him; I hid and was angry, and he went on backsliding in the way of his heart. I have seen his ways, and will heal him; I will also lead him, and restore comforts to him and to his mourners. . . . Peace, peace to him that is far off and to him who is near, says the Lord; and I will heal him." Isa. 57:16-19.

Jacob in his distress was not overwhelmed. He had repented, he had endeavored to atone for the wrong to his brother. And when threatened with death through the wrath of Esau, he looked to God for help. "And He blessed him there." Gen. 32:29. In the power of His might the forgiven one stood up, no longer the supplanter but a prince with God. He had gained not merely deliverance from his outraged brother, but deliverance from himself. The power of evil in his own nature was broken; his character was transformed. In reviewing his life-history Jacob recognized the sustaining power of God.

The Sons of Jacob

The same experience is repeated in the history of Jacob's sons. God does not annul His laws. He does not work contrary to them. He does not undo the work of sin. But He transforms. Through His grace the curse results in blessing.

Of the sons of Jacob, Levi was one of the most cruel and vindictive, one of the two most guilty in the treacherous murder of the Shechemites. Levi's characteristics, reflected in his descendants, incurred for them the decree from God, "I will divide them in Jacob and scatter them in Israel." Gen. 49:7. But repentance produced reformation, and by their faithfulness to God amidst the apostasy of the other tribes, the curse was transformed into a token of highest honor.

"The Lord separated the tribe of Levi to bear the ark of the covenant of the Lord, to stand before the Lord to minister to Him and to bless in His name." Deut. 10:8.

As the appointed ministers of the sanctuary, the Levites received no landed inheritance. They lived together in cities set apart for their use, and received their support from the tithes, gifts, and offerings devoted to God's service. They were the teachers of the people, guests at all their festivities, and everywhere honored as servants and representatives of God. To the whole nation was given the command, "Take heed to yourself that you do not forsake the Levite as long as you live in your land." "Levi has no portion nor inheritance with his brethren; the Lord is his inheritance." Deut. 12:19; 10:9.

By Faith to Conquest

The truth that as a person "thinks in his heart, so is he" (Prov. 23:7), finds another illustration in Israel's experience. On the borders of Canaan the spies, having returned from searching the country, made their report. The beauty and fruitfulness of the land were lost sight of through fear of the difficulties they perceived. The walled cities, the giant warriors, the iron chariots, daunted their faith. Leaving God out of the question, the multitude echoed the decision of the unbelieving spies, "We are not able to go up against the people, for they are stronger than we." Num. 13:31.

Two, however, of the twelve who had viewed the land, reasoned otherwise. "We are well able to overcome it" (vs. 30), they urged, counting God's promise superior to giants, walled cities, or chariots of iron. Though they shared the forty years' wandering with the doubters, Caleb and Joshua entered the Land of Promise. As courageous of heart as when he set out from Egypt, Caleb asked for and received as his portion the stronghold of the giants. In God's strength he drove out the Canaanites, and their vineyards and olive groves became his possession. Though the cowards and rebels perished in the wilderness, the men of faith—Caleb and Joshua— ate of the grapes of Eschol.

No truth does the Bible set forth in clearer light than the peril of even one departure from right—peril both to the wrongdoer and to all whom his influence shall reach. Example has wonderful power, and when cast on the side of the evil tendencies of our nature, it becomes well-nigh irresistible.

The strongest bulwark of vice in our world is not the iniquitous life of the abandoned sinner or the degraded outcast; it is that life which otherwise appears virtuous, honorable, and noble, but in which one sin is fostered, one vice indulged. To a soul struggling in secret against some giant temptation, trembling upon the very verge of the precipice, such an example is one of the most powerful enticements to sin. People who, endowed with high conceptions of life, truth, and honor, willfully transgress one precept of God's holy law, have perverted their noble gifts into a lure to sin. Genius, talent, sympathy, even generous and kindly deeds, may thus become decoys of Satan to entice souls over the precipice of ruin.

This is why God has given so many examples showing the results of even one wrong act. From the sad story of that one sin which "brought death into the world and all our woe, with loss of Eden," to the record of him who for thirty pieces of silver sold the Lord of glory, Bible biography abounds in these examples that are set up as beacons of warning.

Elijah's Failure of Faith

There is warning also in noting the results of yielding even once to human weakness and error, the fruit of letting go of faith.

By one failure of his faith, Elijah cut short his lifework. Heavy was the burden that he had borne in behalf of Israel, faithful had been his warnings against the national idolatry, and deep was his solicitude as during three-and-a-half years of famine he watched and waited for some token of repentance. Alone he stood for God on Mount Carmel. Through the power of faith, idolatry was cast down and the blessed rain testified to the showers of blessing waiting to be poured upon Israel. Then in his weariness and weakness he fled before the threats of Jezebel, and alone in the desert prayed that he might die. His faith had failed. He was not to complete the work he had begun. God told him to anoint another as prophet in his stead.

But God had marked the heart service of His servant. Elijah was not to perish in discouragement and solitude in the wilderness. Not for him the descent to the tomb, but the ascent with God's angels to the presence of His glory.

These life records declare what every human being will one day understand—that sin can bring only shame and loss; that unbelief means failure; but that God's mercy reaches to the deepest depths, and that faith lifts up the repenting soul to share adoption as a son or daughter of God.

The Discipline of Suffering

All who in this world render true service to God or to one another receive a preparatory training in the school of sorrow. The weightier the trust and the higher the service, the closer is the test and the more severe the discipline.

Study the experiences of Joseph and Moses, of Daniel and David. Compare the early history of David with the history of Solomon, and consider the results.

In his youth David was intimately associated with Saul, and his stay at court and his connection with the king's household gave him an insight into the cares and sorrows and perplexities concealed by the glitter and pomp of royalty. He saw how little human glory is worth in bringing peace to the soul. With relief and gladness he returned from the king's court to the sheepfolds and the flocks.

When the jealousy of Saul drove David into the wilderness as a fugitive, cut off from human support, he leaned more heavily upon God. The uncertainty and unrest of the wilderness life, its unceasing peril, its necessity for frequent flight, the character of the men who joined him there, all made stern self-discipline essential. These experiences aroused and developed power to deal with men, sympathy for the oppressed, and hatred of injustice. Through years of waiting and danger, David learned to find in God his comfort, his support, his life. He learned that only by God's power could he be given the throne, only in His wisdom could he rule wisely. It was through training in the school of hardship and sorrow that David was able to make the record—though afterward marred with his great sin— that he "administered judgment and justice to all his people." 2 Sam. 8:15.

The discipline of David's early experience was lacking in that of Solomon. In circumstances, in character, and in life, he seemed favored above all others. Noble in youth, noble in manhood, beloved of his God, Solomon entered on a reign that gave high promise of prosperity and honor. Nations marveled at the knowledge and insight of the man to whom God had given wisdom. But the pride of prosperity brought separation from God. From the joy of divine communion Solomon turned to find satisfaction in the pleasures of sense. Of this experience he says:

"I made my works great, I built myself houses, and planted myself vineyards. I made myself gardens and orchards. . . . I also gathered for myself silver and gold and the special treasure of kings. . . . So I became great, and excelled more than all who were before me in Jerusalem. . . . Then I looked on all the works that my hands had done, and on the labor in which I had toiled; and indeed all was vanity and grasping for the wind.

There was no profit under the sun. . . . I hated life. . . . I hated all my labor in which I had toiled under the sun." Eccl. 2:4-11, 17, 18.

By his own bitter experience Solomon learned the emptiness of a life that seeks its highest good in earthly things. He built altars to heathen gods, only to learn how vain is their promise of rest to the soul. In his later years, wearied and thirsting from earth's broken cisterns, Solomon returned to drink at the fountain of life. By the Spirit of inspiration he recorded the history of his wasted years, with their lessons of warning. And thus, although the seed of his sowing was reaped by his people in harvests of evil, the lifework of Solomon was not wholly lost. For him at last the discipline of suffering accomplished its work.

But with such a dawning, how glorious might have been his life's day had Solomon in his youth learned the lesson that suffering had taught in other lives!

The Testing of Job

For those who love God, those who are "the called according to His purpose" (Rom. 8:28), Bible biography teaches an even higher lesson of the ministry of sorrow. "You are My witnesses, says the Lord, that I am God" (Isa. 43:12)—witnesses that He is good, and that goodness is supreme.

Unselfishness, the principle of God's kingdom, is the principle that Satan hates. He denies its very existence. From the beginning of the great controversy he has endeavored to prove God's principles of action to be selfish, and he deals in the same way with all who serve God. It is the work of Christ and of all who bear His name to disprove Satan's claim.

It was to give an illustration of unselfishness in His own life that Jesus came in the form of humanity. All who accept this principle are to be workers together with Him in demonstrating it in practical life. To choose the right because it is right, to stand for truth at the cost of suffering and sacrifice—"this is the heritage of the servants of the Lord, and their righteousness is from Me, says the Lord." Isa. 54:17.

Very early in the history of the world is given the life record of one over whom this controversy of Satan's was waged.

Of Job the testimony of the Searcher of hearts was, "There is none like him on the earth, a blameless and upright man, who fears God and shuns evil." Against this man Satan brought the scornful charge: "Does

Job fear God for nothing? Have You not made a hedge around him, and around his household, and around all that he has on every side? . . . But stretch out Your hand now and touch all that he has, and he will surely curse You to Your face!"

The Lord said unto Satan, "All that he has is in your power; only do not lay a hand on his person." Job 1:9-12. "Behold he is in your hand, but spare his life." Job 2:6.

Thus permitted, Satan swept away all that Job possessed—flocks and herds, menservants and maidens, sons and daughters—and he "struck Job with painful boils from the sole of his foot to the crown of his head." Job 2:7.

Still another element of bitterness was added to his cup. His friends, seeing in adversity only the retribution of sin, pressed on his bruised and burdened spirit their accusations of wrongdoing.

Seemingly forsaken of heaven and earth, yet holding fast his faith in God and his consciousness of integrity, in anguish and perplexity he cried: "My soul loathes my life." "O that You would hide me in the grave, that You would conceal me, until Your wrath is past, that You would appoint me a set time, and remember me!" Job 10:1; 14:13. "Even though He slay me, yet will I trust Him." Job 13:15. "I know that my Redeemer lives, and He shall stand at last upon the earth; And after my skin is destroyed, this I know, that in my flesh I shall see God, whom I shall see for myself, and my eyes shall behold, and not another." Job 19:25-27. See also Job 19:7-21; 23:3-10.

"When He has tested me," Job said, "I shall come forth as gold." Job 23:10. According to his faith, so it came to pass. By his patient endurance he vindicated his own character and thus the character of Him whose representative he was. And "the Lord restored Job's losses. . . . Indeed the Lord gave Job twice as much as he had before. . . . The Lord blessed the latter days of Job more than his beginning." Job 42:10-12.

Jonathan and John the Baptist

The names of Jonathan and of John the Baptist stand with those who through self-sacrifice entered into the fellowship of Christ's sufferings.

Jonathan was by birth heir to the throne, although he knew he had been set aside by the divine decree. He was a most tender and faithful friend to his rival, David, shielding his life at the peril of his own. He also stood steadfast at his father's side through the dark days of his declining power, and at the end fell at his side. The name of Jonathan is treasured in heaven, and on earth it is a witness to the existence and power of unselfish love.

John the Baptist at his appearance as the Messiah's herald, stirred the nation. From place to place his steps were followed by vast throngs of people of every rank and station. But all was changed when the One came to whom he had borne witness. The crowds followed Jesus, and John's work seemed fast closing. Yet there was no wavering of his faith. "He must increase," he said, "but I must decrease." John 3:30.

Time passed, and the kingdom that John had confidently expected was not established. In Herod's dungeon, cut off from life-giving air and the desert freedom, he waited and watched.

There was no display of swords, no rending of prison doors; but the healing of the sick, the preaching of the gospel, the uplifting of human souls, testified to Christ's mission.

Alone in the dungeon, seeing the direction his path, like his Master's, tended, John accepted the trust—fellowship with Christ in sacrifice. Heaven's messengers ministered to him as he went to the grave. The intelligences of the universe, fallen and unfallen, witnessed his vindication of unselfish service.

And in all the generations that have passed since then, suffering souls have been sustained by the testimony of John's life. In the dungeon, on the scaffold, in the flames, men and women through centuries of darkness have been strengthened by the memory of him of whom Christ declared, "Among those born of women there has not risen one greater than John the Baptist." Matt. 11:11.

Poetry
and Song

The earliest as well as the most sublime of poetic utterances known in literature are found in the Scriptures. Before the oldest of the world's poets had sung, the shepherd of Midian recorded those words of God to Job—in their majesty unequaled, unapproached, by the loftiest productions of human genius:

"Where were you when I laid the foundations of the earth? . . .
Or who shut in the sea with doors,
When it burst forth; . . .
When I made the clouds its garment,
And thick darkness its swaddling band;
When I fixed My limit for it,
And set bars and doors;
When I said, This far you may come, but no farther,
And here your proud waves must stop!" Job 38:4-11.
See also Job 38:12-27; 38:31, 32.

For beauty of expression read also the description of springtime, from the Song of Songs:

"Lo, the winter is past,
 The rain is over and gone.
The flowers appear on the earth;
The time of singing has come,
And the voice of the turtledove is heard in our land.
The fig tree puts forth her green figs,
And the vines with tender grapes
Give a good smell.
Rise up, my love, my fair one, and come away!"
Song of Sol. 2:11-13.

And not inferior in beauty is Balaam's unwilling prophecy of blessing to Israel (Num. 23:7-23; 24:4-6; 24:16-19).

The melody of praise is the atmosphere of heaven, and when heaven comes in touch with the earth, there is music and song—"thanksgiving and the voice of melody." Isa. 51:3.

Above the newly created earth, as it lay fair and unblemished under the smile of God, "the morning stars sang together, and all the sons of God shouted for joy." Job 38:7. So human hearts, in sympathy with heaven, have responded to God's goodness in notes of praise. Many of the events of human history have been linked with song.

The earliest song recorded in the Bible from human lips was that glorious outburst of thanksgiving by the hosts of Israel at the Red Sea:

"I will sing to the Lord, for He has triumphed gloriously!
The horse and its rider He has thrown into the sea!
The Lord is my strength and song,
And He has become my salvation;
He is my God, and I will praise Him;
My father's God, and I will exalt Him." Exod. 15:1, 2.
See also Exod. 15:6-11, 18-21.

Great have been the blessings received by human beings in response to songs of praise. The few words recounting an experience of the wilderness journey of Israel have a lesson worthy of our thought: "They went to Beer, which is the well where the Lord said to Moses, 'Gather the people together, and I will give them water.'" Num. 21:16. Then Israel sang this song:

"Spring up, O well! All of you sing to it.
The well, the leaders sank,
Dug by the nation's nobles,
By the lawgiver, with their staves." Num. 21:17, 18.

How often in spiritual experience is this history repeated! How often by words of holy song are unsealed in the soul the springs of penitence and faith, of hope and love and joy!

With songs of praise the armies of Israel went forth to the great deliverance under Jehoshaphat. To Jehoshaphat had come the news of threatened war. "A great multitude is coming against you," was the message—"the people of Moab, and the people of Ammon, and others with them besides." "And Jehoshaphat feared, and set himself to seek the Lord, and proclaimed a fast throughout all Judah." And Jehoshaphat, standing in the temple court before his people, poured out his soul in prayer, confessing Israel's helplessness and pleading God's promise. "We have no power against this great multitude that is coming against us," he said, "nor do we know what to do, but our eyes are upon You." 2 Chron. 20:2, 1, 3, 12.

Then the Spirit of the Lord came upon Jahaziel, a Levite, and he said, "Listen, all you of Judah, and you inhabitants of Jerusalem, and you, King Jehoshaphat! Thus says the Lord to you, 'Do not be afraid nor dismayed because of this great multitude, for the battle is not yours, but God's. . . . You will not need to fight in this battle. Position yourselves, stand still and see the salvation of the Lord. . . . Do not fear or be dismayed; tomorrow go out against them, for the Lord is with you.'" 2 Chron. 20:14-17.

"So they rose early in the morning, and went out into the Wilderness of Tekoa." 2 Chron. 20:20. Ahead of the army went singers, lifting their voices in praise to God—praising Him for the victory promised.

Four days later the army returned to Jerusalem, laden with the spoil of their enemies, singing praise for the victory won.

Through song, David, amidst the vicissitudes of his ever-changing life, held communion with heaven. How moving are his experiences as a young shepherd reflected in the words:

"The Lord is my Shepherd; I shall not want.
He maketh me to lie down in green pastures:

He leadeth me beside the still waters. . . .
Though I walk through the valley of the shadow of death,
I will fear no evil: for Thou art with me;
Thy rod and Thy staff they comfort me." Ps. 23:1-4, KJV.

In his manhood a hunted fugitive, finding refuge in the rocks and caves of the wilderness, he wrote:

"O God, You are my God; early will I seek You;
My soul thirsts for You; my flesh longs for You
In a dry and thirsty land where there is no water. . . .
You have been my help,
Therefore in the shadow of Your wings I will rejoice."
Ps. 63: 1, 7.
See also Ps. 42:11; 27:1.

The same trust is breathed in David's words written when, as a dethroned and crownless king, he fled from Jerusalem at the rebellion of Absalom. Spent with grief and the weariness of his flight, he and his company had stopped beside the Jordan for a few hours' rest. He was awakened by the summons to immediate flight. The deep and swift-flowing stream must be crossed in the darkness by that whole company of men, women, and little children, for approaching them rapidly were the forces of the traitor son.

In that hour of darkest trial, David sang:

"I cried to the Lord with my voice,
And He heard me from His holy hill. . . .
I lay down and slept; I awoke, for the Lord sustained me.
I will not be afraid of ten thousands of people
Who have set themselves against me all around." Ps. 3:4-6.

After his great sin, in the anguish of remorse and self-abhorrence, he still turned to God as his best friend:

"Have mercy upon me, O God, according to Your lovingkindness;

According to the multitude of Your tender mercies, blot out my transgressions. . . .
Purge me with hyssop, and I shall be clean;
Wash me, and I shall be whiter than snow." Ps. 51:1-7.

In his long life, David found on earth no resting place. "We are aliens and pilgrims before You," he said, "as were all our fathers; our days on earth are as a shadow, and without hope." 1 Chron. 29:15. "God is our refuge and strength, a very present help in trouble. Therefore we will not fear, even though the earth be removed, and though the mountains be carried into the midst of the sea." See Ps. 46:4-7.

Jesus in His earthly life met temptation with a song. Often when enemies spoke sharp, stinging words, often when the atmosphere about Him was heavy with gloom, dissatisfaction, distrust, or oppressive fear, His song of faith and holy cheer was heard.

On that last sad night of the Passover supper, as He was about to go forth to betrayal and death, His voice was lifted in the psalm:

"Blessed be the name of the Lord
From this time forth and forevermore!
From the rising of the sun to its going down
The Lord's name is to be praised." Ps. 113:2, 3. See also
Ps.116:1-8.

In earth's last great crisis, God's light will shine brightest amidst the deepening shadows. The song of hope and trust will be heard in clearest and loftiest strains.

"Those of steadfast mind
You keep in perfect peace—
In peace because they trust in You.
Trust in the Lord forever,
For in the Lord God you have an everlasting rock." Isa. 26:1-4,
NRSV.

The Power of Song

The history of the songs of the Bible is full of suggestion regarding the uses and benefits of music and song. Music is often perverted to serve purposes of evil, and it thus becomes one of the most alluring agencies of temptation. But, rightly employed, it is a precious gift of God, designed to uplift the thoughts to high and noble themes, to inspire and elevate the soul.

As the children of Israel, journeying through the wilderness, cheered their way by the music of sacred song, so God wants His children today to gladden their pilgrim life. There are few means more effective for fixing His words in the memory than repeating them in song. And such song has wonderful power. It has power to subdue rude and uncultivated natures, power to quicken thought and awaken sympathy, power to promote harmony of action and banish the gloom and foreboding that destroy courage and weaken effort. It is one of the most effective means of impressing the heart with spiritual truth.

The value of song as a means of education should never be lost sight of. If songs are sung in the home—songs that are sweet and pure—there will be fewer words of censure and more of cheerfulness, hope, and joy. If there is singing in the school, the students will be drawn closer to God, to their teachers, and to one another.

As a part of religious service, singing is as much an act of worship as is prayer. Indeed, many a song is prayer. If children are taught to realize this, they will think more of the meaning of the words they sing and will be more susceptible to their power.

As our Redeemer leads us to the threshold of the Infinite, flushed with the glory of God, we may catch the themes of praise and thanksgiving from the heavenly choir around the throne; and as the echo of the angels' song is awakened in our earthly homes, hearts will be drawn closer to the heavenly singers. Heaven's communion begins on earth. We learn here the keynote of its praise.

Chapter 18

Mysteries
of the Bible

No finite mind can fully comprehend the character or the works of the Infinite One. We cannot by searching find out God. To the strongest and most highly cultured minds, as well as to the weakest and most ignorant, that holy Being must remain clothed in mystery. "Clouds and darkness surround Him; righteousness and justice are the foundation of His throne." Ps. 97:2. We can understand as much of His purposes as we are capable of comprehending; beyond this we may still trust the hand that is omnipotent, the heart that is full of love.

The Word of God, like the character of its Author, presents mysteries that can never be fully comprehended by finite beings. But God has given in the Scriptures sufficient evidence of their divine authority. His own existence, His character, the truthfulness of His word, are established by testimony that appeals to our reason—and this testimony is abundant. True, He has not removed the possibility of doubt; faith must rest upon evidence, not demonstration. Those who wish to doubt have opportunity, but those who desire to know the truth find ample ground for faith.

We have no reason to doubt God's Word because we cannot understand the mysteries of His providence. In the natural world we are constantly surrounded with wonders beyond our grasp. Should we then be surprised to find in the spiritual world mysteries that we cannot fathom? The difficulty lies solely in the weakness and narrowness of the human mind.

Strong Evidence of Inspiration

The mysteries of the Bible, so far from being an argument against it, are among the strongest evidences of its divine inspiration. If it contained no account of God but that which we could understand, if His greatness and majesty could be grasped by finite minds, then the Bible would not bear the unmistakable evidences of divinity. The greatness of its themes should inspire faith in it as the Word of God.

The Bible unfolds truth with a simplicity and an adaptation to the needs and longings of the human heart that has astonished and charmed the most highly cultivated minds, while to the humble and uncultured it also makes plain the way of life. "Whoever walks the road, although a fool, shall not go astray." Isa. 35:8. The more we search the Bible, the deeper is our conviction that it is the Word of the living God, and human reason bows before the majesty of divine revelation.

God intends that to the earnest seeker the truths of His Word shall be ever unfolding. While "the secret things belong to the Lord our God," "those things which are revealed belong to us and to our children." Deut. 29:29. The idea that certain portions of the Bible cannot be understood has led to neglect of some of its most important truths. The fact needs to be emphasized, and often repeated, that the mysteries of the Bible are not such because God has endeavored to conceal truth, but because our own weakness or ignorance makes us incapable of understanding or appropriating truth. The limitation is not in His purpose but in our capacity. Of those very portions of Scripture often passed by as impossible to be understood, God desires us to understand as much as our minds are capable of receiving. "All Scripture is given by inspiration of God," that we may be "thoroughly equipped for every good work." 2 Tim. 3:16, 17.

It is impossible for any human mind to exhaust even one truth or promise of the Bible. One person catches the glory from one point of view, another from another point, yet we can discern only gleamings. The full radiance is beyond our vision.

Study of the Bible Gives New Power

As we contemplate the great things of God's Word, its breadth and depth pass our knowledge. It stretches out before us as a boundless, shoreless sea.

Such study has vitalizing power. The mind and heart acquire new strength, new life. This experience is the highest evidence of the divine authorship of the Bible. We receive God's Word as food for the soul, through the same evidence by which we receive bread as food for the body. Bread supplies the need of our nature; we know by experience that it produces blood and bone and brain.

Apply the same test to the Bible. When its principles have actually become the elements of character, what has been the result? What changes have been made in the life? "Old things have passed away; behold, all things have become new." 2 Cor. 5:17. In its power, men and women have broken the chains of sinful habit. They have renounced selfishness. The profane have become reverent, the drunken sober, the profligate pure. Souls that have borne the likeness of Satan have been transformed into the image of God. This change is itself the miracle of miracles. A change wrought by the Word is one of the deepest mysteries of the Word. We cannot understand it; we can only believe that it is, as declared by the Scriptures, "Christ in you, the hope of glory." Col. 1:27.

A knowledge of this mystery furnishes a key to every other. It opens to the soul the treasures of the universe, the possibilities of infinite development.

And this development is gained through the constant unfolding of the character of God—the glory and the mystery of the written Word. If it were possible for us to attain to a full understanding of God and His Word, there would be for us no further discovery of truth, no greater knowledge, no further development. God would cease to be supreme, and human beings would cease to advance. Thank God, it is not so. Since God is infinite, and in Him are all the treasures of wisdom, we may through all eternity ever search, ever learn, yet never exhaust the riches of His wisdom, His goodness, or His power.

Chapter 19

History
and Prophecy

The Bible is the most ancient and comprehensive history that exists. It came fresh from the fountain of eternal truth, and throughout the ages a divine hand has preserved its purity. It lights up the far-distant past where human research seeks in vain to penetrate. In God's Word only do we behold the power that laid the foundations of the earth and that stretched out the heavens. Here only do we find an authentic account of the origin of nations. Here only is given a history of our race unsullied by human pride or prejudice.

In the annals of human history the growth of nations, the rise and fall of empires, appear as dependent on the will and prowess of mortals. The shaping of events seems, to a great degree, to be determined by human power, ambition, or caprice. But in the Word of God the curtain is drawn aside, and we see, behind, above, and through all the play and counterplay of human interests and power and passions, the agencies of the all-merciful One, silently, patiently working out the counsels of His own will.

The Bible reveals the true philosophy of history. In those words of matchless beauty and tenderness spoken by the apostle Paul to the sages of Athens is set forth God's purpose in the creation and distribution of races and nations: "From one ancestor He made all nations to inhabit the whole earth, and He allotted the times of their existence and the boundaries of the places where they would live, so that they would search for God and perhaps grope for Him and find Him." Acts 17:26, 27, NRSV. In the creation it was His purpose that the earth be inhabited by beings whose existence should be a blessing to themselves and to one another, and an honor to their Creator. All who choose to may identify themselves with this purpose. Of them it is spoken, "This people have I formed for Myself; they shall declare My praise." Isa. 43:21.

God has revealed in His law the principles that underlie all true prosperity both of nations and of individuals. "This is your wisdom and your understanding," Moses declared to the Israelites of the law of God. Deut. 4:6. The blessings thus assured to Israel are, on the same conditions and in the same degree, assured to every nation and every person under the broad heavens.

Only God Can Give Power to Rulers of Nations
The power exercised by every ruler on the earth is Heaven-imparted, and success depends on the use of the power thus bestowed. To each the words spoken to Nebuchadnezzar of old are the lesson of life: "Break off your sins by being righteous, and your iniquities by showing mercy to the poor. Perhaps there may be a lengthening of your prosperity." Dan. 4:27.

To understand these things, to recognize the outworking of these principles in the manifestation of His power who "removes kings, and raises up kings" (Dan. 2: 21), is to understand the philosophy of history.

In the Word of God only is this clearly set forth. Here it is shown that the strength of nations, as of individuals, is not found in the opportunities or facilities that appear to make them invincible, nor is it found in their boasted greatness. It is measured by the fidelity with which they fulfill God's purpose.

Ancient Babylon
An illustration of this truth is found in the history of ancient Babylon. To King Nebuchadnezzar the true object of national government was represented under the figure of a great tree whose height "reached to the heavens, and it could be seen to the ends of all the earth. The leaves were lovely, its fruit abundant, and in it was food for all." Under its shadow lived the

beasts of the field, and among its branches the birds of the air had their nests. Dan. 4:11, 12. This representation shows the character of a government that fulfills God's purpose, a government that protects and upbuilds the nation.

God exalted Babylon that it might fulfill this purpose. Prosperity attended the nation until it reached a height of wealth and power that has never been equaled—fitly represented in the Scriptures by the inspired symbol, a "head of gold." Dan. 2:38.

But the king failed to recognize the power that had exalted him. Nebuchadnezzar, in the pride of his heart, said: "Is not this great Babylon, that I have built for a royal dwelling by my mighty power and for the honor of my majesty?" Dan. 4:30.

Instead of being a protector of its people, Babylon became a proud and cruel oppressor. The words of Inspiration picturing the cruelty and greed of rulers in Israel reveal the secret of Babylon's fall and of the fall of many other kingdoms since the world began: "With force and cruelty you have ruled them." Eze. 34:3, 4.

To the ruler of Babylon came the sentence of the divine Watcher: King Nebuchadnezzar, "to you it is spoken: The kingdom has departed from you!" Dan. 4:31.

"Babylon, the glory of kingdoms,
The beauty of the Chaldees' pride,
Will be as when God overthrew Sodom and Gomorrah." Isa. 13:19.

The Rise and Fall of World Empires

Every nation that has come on the stage of action has been permitted to occupy its place on the earth that it might be seen whether it would fulfill the purpose of "the Watcher and the Holy One." Prophecy has traced the rise and fall of the world's great empires—Babylon, Medo-Persia, Greece, and Rome. With each of these, as with nations of less power, history repeated itself. Each had its period of test. Each failed. Its glory faded, its power departed, and its place was occupied by another.

While the nations rejected God's principles, and in this rejection ruined themselves, it was still seen that the divine, overruling purpose was working through all their movements.

This lesson is taught in a wonderful symbolic representation given to the prophet Ezekiel during his exile in the land of the Chaldeans. The vision was given at a time when Ezekiel was weighed down with sorrowful memories and troubled forebodings. The land of his fathers was desolate. Jerusalem was depopulated. The prophet himself was a stranger in a land where ambition and cruelty reigned supreme. As on every hand he beheld tyranny and wrong, his soul was distressed, and he mourned day and night. But the symbols presented to him revealed a power above that of earthly rulers.

Ezekiel and the Whirlwind

On the banks of the river Chebar, Ezekiel saw a whirlwind seeming to come from the north, "a great cloud with raging fire engulfing itself; and brightness was all around it and radiating out of its midst like the color of amber." A number of wheels, intersecting one another, were moved by four living beings. High above all these "was something like a throne, in appearance like sapphire; and seated above the likeness of the throne was something that seemed like a human form." "The cherubim appeared to have the form of a human hand under their wings." Eze. 1:4, 26; 10:8, NRSV. The wheels were so complicated in arrangement that at first sight they appeared to be in confusion, but they moved in perfect harmony. Heavenly beings, sustained and guided by the hand beneath the wings of the cherubim, were impelling these wheels. Above them, on the sapphire throne, was the Eternal One, and round about the throne a rainbow, the emblem of divine mercy.

As the wheel-like complications were under the guidance of the hand beneath the wings of the cherubim, so the complicated play of human events is under divine control. Amidst the strife and tumult of nations, He that sits above the cherubim still guides the affairs of earth.

The history of nations that one after another have occupied their allotted time and place, speaks to us. To every nation and to every person God has assigned a place in His great plan. Today individuals and nations are being measured by Him who makes no mistake. All are by their own choice deciding their destiny, and God is overruling all for the accomplishment of His purposes.

The history that the great I AM has marked out in His Word, uniting link after link in the prophetic chain, from eternity in the past to eternity in the future, tells us where we are today in the procession of the ages, and what may be expected in the time to come. All that prophecy has foretold as coming to pass, until the present time, has been traced on the pages of history, and we may be assured that all which is yet to come will be fulfilled in its order.

On the Threshold of Great Events

The final overthrow of all earthly dominions is plainly foretold in the Word of truth. The message is given in the sentence from God that was pronounced upon the last king of Israel: "Thus says the Lord God: Remove the turban, and take off the crown: . . . exalt the humble, and humble the exalted. . . . Overthrown, overthrown, I will make it overthrown! It shall be no longer, until He comes whose right it is, and I will give it to Him." Eze. 21:26, 27.

The crown removed from Israel passed successively to the kingdoms of Babylon, Medo-Persia, Greece, and Rome. God says, "It shall be no longer, until He comes whose right it is, and I will give it to Him."

That time is at hand. Today the signs of the times declare that we are standing on the threshold of great and solemn events. Everything in our world is in agitation. Before our eyes the Savior's prophecy of the events preceding His coming is being fulfilled: "You will hear of wars and rumors of wars. . . . Nation will rise against nation, and kingdom against kingdom. There will be famines, and pestilences, and earthquakes in various places." Matt. 24:6, 7.

The present is a time of overwhelming interest to all living. Rulers and statesmen, people who occupy positions of trust and authority, thinking men and women of all classes, have their attention fixed on the events taking place about us. They are watching the strained, restless relations that exist among the nations. They observe the intensity that is taking possession of every earthly element, and they recognize that something great and decisive is about to take place—that the world is on the verge of a stupendous crisis.

Angels are now restraining the winds of strife that they may not blow until the world shall be warned of its coming doom. But a storm is gathering, ready to burst upon the earth, and when God shall command His angels to loose the winds, there will be such a scene of strife as no pen can picture.

The Final Scenes of Earth's History

The Bible, and the Bible only, gives a correct view of these things. Here are revealed the great final scenes in the history of our world, events that already are casting their shadows.

"They have transgressed the laws, changed the ordinance, broken the everlasting covenant. Therefore the curse has devoured the earth, and those that dwell in it are desolate." Isa. 24:5, 6.

"I looked on the earth, and lo, it was waste and void; and to the heavens, and they had no light. I looked on the mountains, and lo, they were quaking, and all the hills moved to and fro. I looked, and lo, there was no one at all, and all the birds of the air had fled. I looked, and lo, the fruitful land was a desert, and all its cities were laid in ruins." Jer. 4:23-26, NRSV.

"Come, My people, enter your chambers, and shut your doors behind you; hide yourself, as it were, for a little moment, until the indignation is past." Isa. 26:20.

"Because you have made the Lord, who is my refuge,
Even the Most High, your habitation,
No evil shall befall you,
Nor shall any plague come near your dwelling." Ps. 91:9, 10.
See also Ps. 50:1-4; Micah 4:10-12; Jer. 30:17, 18;
Isa. 25:9, 8; 30:20-22; 60:18; 54:14.

The prophets to whom these great scenes were revealed longed to understand their import. They "inquired and searched carefully: . . . searching what, or what manner of time the Spirit of Christ who was in them was indicating. . . . To them it was revealed that, not to themselves, but to us they were ministering the things which now have been reported to you—things which angels desire to look into." 1 Peter 1:10-12.

To those who are standing on the very verge of their fulfillment, of what deep moment, what living interest, are these delineations of the things to come—events for which, since our first parents turned their steps from Eden, God's children have watched and waited, longed and prayed!

Things of True Value

At this time, as before the world's first destruction, men and women today are absorbed in the pleasures and pursuits of sense. They have lost sight of the unseen and eternal. They are sacrificing imperishable riches for the things that perish with the using. Their minds need to be uplifted, their views of life broadened. They need to be aroused from the lethargy of worldly dreaming.

From the rise and fall of nations, as made plain in the Scriptures, they need to learn how worthless is mere outward and worldly glory. Babylon, with all its power and magnificence—power and magnificence which to the people of that day seemed so stable and enduring—how completely has it disappeared! As "the flower of the grass" it has perished. So perishes all that does not have God for its foundation. Only that which is bound up with His purpose and expresses His character can endure. His principles are the only steadfast things our world knows.

It is these great truths that old and young need to learn. We need to study the working out of God's purpose in the history of nations and in the revelation of things to come, that we may estimate the true value of things seen and things unseen and may learn the true aim of life. Learning here the principles of His kingdom and becoming its subjects and citizens, we may be prepared to possess it at His coming.

The day is at hand. For the lessons to be learned, the work to be done, the transformation of character to be effected, the time remaining is all too brief.

"'None of My words will be postponed any more, but the word which I speak will be done,' says the Lord God." Eze. 12:27, 28.

Bible Teaching and Study

In childhood, youth, and adulthood, Jesus studied the Scriptures. As a little child He was taught daily at His mother's knee from the scrolls of the prophets. In His youth the early morning and the evening twilight often found Him alone on the mountainside or among the trees of the forest, spending a quiet hour in prayer and the study of God's Word. During His ministry His intimate acquaintance with the Scriptures testifies to His diligence in their study. And since He gained knowledge as we may gain it, His wonderful mental and spiritual power is a testimony to the value of the Bible as a means of education.

Teach Children From an Early Age

In giving His Word our heavenly Father did not overlook the children. In all that mortals have written, where can anything be found that has such a hold on the heart, anything so well adapted to awaken the interest of little ones, as the stories of the Bible?

In these simple stories may be made plain the great principles of the law of God. Thus by illustrations best suited to a child's comprehension, parents and teachers may begin very early to fulfill the Lord's injunction concerning His precepts: "You shall teach them diligently to your children, and shall talk of them when you sit in your house, when you walk by the way, when you lie down, and when you rise up." Deut. 6:7.

The use of object lessons, maps, and pictures, will be an aid in explaining these lessons and fixing them in the memory. Parents and teachers should constantly seek for improved methods. The teaching of the Bible should have our freshest thought, our best methods, and our most earnest effort.

In arousing and strengthening a love for Bible study, much depends on the period of worship. Morning and evening worship should be the sweetest and most helpful time of the day. Into this time no troubled, unkind thoughts are to intrude. Parents and children assemble to meet with Jesus, and to invite holy angels into the home. The services should be brief and full of life, adapted to the occasion, and varied from time to time. Let all join in the Bible reading and learn and often repeat God's law. It will add to the interest of the children if sometimes they are permitted to select the reading. Question them about it, and let them ask questions. Mention anything that will serve to illustrate its meaning. When the service is not too lengthy, let the little ones take part in prayer and join in song, even if it is only a single verse.

To make such a service what it should be, thought should be given to preparation. And parents should take time daily for Bible study with their children. No doubt it will require effort and planning and some sacrifice to accomplish this, but the effort will be richly repaid.

In order to interest our children in the Bible, we ourselves must be interested in it. To awaken in them a love for its study, we must love it. Our instruction to them will have only the weight of influence given it by our own example and spirit.

God called Abraham to be a teacher of His word, and chose him to be the father of a great nation, because He saw that Abraham would instruct his children and his household in the principles of His law. And that which gave power to Abraham's teaching was the influence of his own life. His great household consisted of more than a thousand people, many of them heads of families, and not a few who were newly converted from heathenism. Such a household required a firm hand at the helm. No weak, vacillating methods would suffice.

Of Abraham God said, "I know him, that he will command his children and his household after him." Gen. 18:19, KJV. Yet his authority was exercised with such wisdom and tenderness that hearts were won. Abraham's influence extended beyond his own household. Wherever he pitched his tent, he set up beside it an altar for sacrifice and worship. When the tent was removed, the altar remained, and many a roving Canaanite, whose knowledge of God had been gained from the life of Abraham His servant, tarried at that altar to offer sacrifice to Jehovah.

No less effective today will be the teaching of God's Word when it finds as faithful a reflection in the teacher's life.

All Must Give Account of Themselves

It is not enough to know what others have thought or learned about the Bible. Everyone must in the judgment give account of himself or herself to God, and each should now learn personally what is truth. But in order to do effective study, the interest of the pupil must be enlisted. This is a matter not to be lost sight of, especially by teachers who have to deal with children and young people who differ widely in disposition, training, and habits of thought. In teaching the Bible to children, we may gain much by observing the bent of their minds, discovering the things in which they are interested, and arousing their interest to see what the Bible says about these things. He who created us, with our various aptitudes, has in His Word given something for everyone. As the students see that the lessons of the Bible apply to their own lives, teach them to look to it as a counselor.

Help them also to appreciate its wonderful beauty. Many books of no real value—books that are exciting and unhealthful—are recommended, or at least permitted to be used, because of their supposed literary value. Why should we direct our children to drink of these polluted streams when they may have free access to the pure fountains of the Word of God? The Bible has a fullness, a strength, a depth of meaning, that is inexhaustible. Encourage the children and youth to seek out its treasures both of thought and of expression.

As the beauty of these precious things attracts their minds, a softening, subduing power will touch their hearts. They will be drawn to Him who has thus revealed Himself to them. And there are few who will not desire to know more of His works and ways. Students of the Bible should be taught to approach it in the spirit of a learner. We are to search its pages, not for proof to sustain our opinions, but to know what God says.

A true knowledge of the Bible can be gained only through the aid of that Spirit by whom the Word was given. And in order to gain this knowledge we must live by it. All that God's Word commands, we are to obey. All that it promises, we may claim. The life that it enjoins is the life that, through its power, we are to live. Only as the Bible is thus held can it be studied effectively.

The study of the Bible demands our most diligent effort and persevering thought. As the miner digs for the golden treasure in the earth, so earnestly, persistently must we seek for the treasure of God's Word.

In daily study the verse-by-verse method is often most helpful. Let the student take one verse, and concentrate on ascertaining the thought that God has put into that verse for him or her. Then dwell on the thought until it becomes one's own. A single passage thus studied until its significance is clear is of more value than the perusal of many chapters with no definite purpose in view and no positive instruction gained.

One of the chief causes of mental inefficiency and moral weakness is the lack of concentration for worthy ends. We pride ourselves on the wide distribution of literature, but the multiplication of books, even books that in themselves are not harmful, may be a positive evil. With the immense tide of printed matter constantly pouring from the press, old and young form the habit of reading hastily and superficially, and the mind loses its power of connected and vigorous thought.

Furthermore, a large share of the periodicals and books that are overspreading the land like a plague, are not merely commonplace, idle, and enervating, they are unclean and degrading. Their effect is not merely to intoxicate and ruin the mind, but to corrupt and destroy the soul. The mind, the heart, that is indolent and aimless falls an easy prey to evil. It is on diseased, lifeless organisms that fungus takes root. It is the idle mind that is Satan's workshop. Let the mind be directed to high and holy ideals, let the life have a noble aim, an absorbing purpose, and evil finds little foothold.

Teach the youth, then, to give close study to the Word of God. Received into the soul, it will prove a mighty barricade against temptation. "Your word," the psalmist declares, "have I hid in my heart, that I might not sin against You." "By the word of Your lips, I have kept myself from the paths of the destroyer." Ps. 119:11; 17:4.

Compare Scripture With Scripture

The Bible is its own expositor. Scripture is to be compared with scripture. Students should learn to view the Word as a whole, and to see the relation of its parts. They should gain a knowledge of its grand central theme, of God's original purpose for the world, of the rise of the great controversy, and of the work of redemption. They should understand the nature of the two principles that are contending for supremacy, and should learn to trace their working through the records of history and prophecy, to the great consummation. They should see how this controversy enters into every phase of human experience, how in every act of life a person reveals one or the other of the two antagonistic motives, and that they are even now deciding on which side of the controversy they will be found.

Every part of the Bible is given by inspiration of God and is profitable. The Old Testament no less than the New should receive attention. As we study the Old Testament we shall find living springs bubbling up where the careless reader discerns only a desert.

The book of Revelation, in connection with the book of Daniel, especially demands study. Every God-fearing teacher should consider how most clearly to present the gospel that our Savior came in person to make known to His servant John—"The Revelation of Jesus Christ, which God gave Him, to show His servants things which must shortly take place." Rev. 1:1.

When real love for the Bible is awakened, and students begin to realize how vast is the field and how precious its treasure, they will desire to seize every opportunity for acquainting themselves with God's Word. Its study will not be restricted to any special time or place. This continuous study is one of the best means of cultivating a love for the Scriptures. Encourage students to keep their Bibles always with them. As they have opportunity, let them read a text and meditate on it, thus gaining some precious thought from the treasure house of truth.

The great motive powers of the soul are faith, hope, and love, and it is to these that Bible study, rightly pursued, appeals. The outward beauty of the Bible, the beauty of imagery and expression, is but the setting, as it were, for its real treasure—the beauty of holiness. In its record of the men and women who walked with God, we may catch glimpses of His glory. In the One "altogether lovely" we behold Him of whom all beauty of earth and heaven is but a dim reflection. As students of the Bible behold the Redeemer, there is awakened in the soul the mysterious power of faith, adoration, and love. The gaze is fixed upon Christ, and the beholders grow into the likeness of that which they adore.

The springs of heavenly peace and joy unsealed in the soul by the words of Inspiration will become a mighty river of influence to bless all who come within its reach. Let young Christians of today, those who are growing up with the Bible in their hands, receive its life-giving energy, and what streams of blessing will flow forth to the world!

Chapter 21

Study of Physiology

Since the mind and the soul find expression through the body, both mental and spiritual vigor are in great degree dependent on physical strength and activity. Whatever promotes physical health promotes the development of a strong mind and a well-balanced character. Without health no one can as distinctly understand or as completely fulfill his or her obligations to oneself, to other persons, or to the Creator. Therefore the health should be as faithfully guarded as the character. A knowledge of physiology and hygiene should be the basis of all educational effort.

Though the facts of physiology are now generally understood, there is an alarming indifference in regard to the principles of health. Even of those who have a knowledge of these principles, few put them into practice.

The youth, in the freshness and vigor of life, little realize the value of their abounding energy. A treasure more precious than gold, more essential to advancement than learning or rank or riches—how lightly it is held, how rashly squandered! Many men and women, sacrificing health in the struggle for riches or power, have almost reached the object of their desire, only to fall helpless, while others, possessing superior physical endurance, grasp the longed-for prize! Through morbid conditions, the result of neglecting the laws of health, many have been led into evil practices, to the sacrifice of every hope for this world and the next.

In the study of physiology, pupils should be led to see the value of physical energy and how it can be preserved and developed to contribute in the highest degree to success in life's great struggle.

Teach Children to Live Healthfully

Children should be taught, in simple, easy lessons, the rudiments of physiology and hygiene. The work should be begun by the mother in the home and should be faithfully carried forward in the school. As the students advance in years, instruction in this line should be continued until they are qualified to care for the house they live in. They should understand the importance of guarding against disease by preserving the vigor of every organ. They also should be taught how to deal with common diseases and accidents. Every school should give instruction in both physiology and hygiene.

There are matters not usually included in the study of physiology that should be considered—matters of far greater value to the student than many of the technicalities commonly taught under this subject. As the foundation principle of all education in these lines, the young should be taught that the laws of nature are the laws of God—as truly divine as are the precepts of the Decalogue. God has written on every nerve, muscle, and fiber of the body the laws that govern our physical organism. Every careless or willful violation of these laws is a sin against our Creator.

The influence of the mind on the body, as well as of the body on the mind, should be emphasized. The electric power of the brain, promoted by mental activity, vitalizes the whole system, and is thus an invaluable aid in resisting disease. This should be made plain. The power of the will and the importance of self-control, both in the preservation and in the recovery of health, should be emphasized. Likewise, the depressing and even ruinous effect of anger, discontent, selfishness, or impurity should be shown. On the other hand, the marvelous life-giving power to be found in cheerfulness, unselfishness, and gratitude should be emphasized.

There is a physiological truth in the scripture, "A merry [rejoicing] heart does good, like medicine." Prov. 17:22.

As the mechanism of the body is studied, attention should be directed to its wonderful adaptation of means to ends, the harmonious action and dependence of the various organs. As the interest of the students is thus awakened, and they are led to see the importance of physical culture, much can be done by the teacher to secure proper development and right habits.

Correct Posture and Respiration

Among the first things to be aimed at should be a correct position, both in sitting and in standing. God made humans upright, and He desires them to possess not only the physical but the mental and moral benefit, the grace and dignity and self-possession, the courage and self-reliance, that an erect bearing greatly tends to promote. Let the teacher give instruction on this point by example and precept. Show what a correct position is, and insist that it be maintained.

Next in importance to right position are respiration and vocal culture. The one who sits and stands erect is more likely than others to breathe properly. But the teacher should impress upon students the importance of deep breathing. Show how the healthy action of the respiratory organs, assisting the circulation of the blood, invigorates the whole system, excites the appetite, promotes digestion, and induces sound, sweet sleep. This not only refreshes the body but soothes and tranquilizes the mind. Let exercises in deep breathing be given, and see that the habit becomes established.

The training of the voice has an important place in physical development, since it tends to expand and strengthen the lungs, and thus to ward off disease. To ensure correct delivery in reading and speaking, see that the abdominal muscles have full play in breathing and that the respiratory organs are unrestricted. Let the strain come on the muscles of the abdomen rather than on those of the throat. Great weariness and serious disease of the throat and lungs may thus be prevented. Careful attention should be given to securing distinct articulation, smooth, well-modulated tones, and a not-too-rapid delivery. This will not only promote health but will add greatly to the agreeableness and efficiency of the student's work.

In the study of hygiene the earnest teacher will improve every opportunity to show the necessity of perfect cleanliness both in personal habits and in one's surroundings. The value of a daily bath in promoting health and in stimulating mental action, should be emphasized. Attention should be given also to sunlight and ventilation, the hygiene of the sleeping room and the kitchen. Teach students that a healthful sleeping room, a thoroughly clean kitchen, and a tastefully arranged, wholesomely supplied table, will go further toward securing the happiness of the family than any amount of expensive furnishings. That "life is more than food, and the body is more than clothing" (Luke 12:23) is a lesson no less needed now than when first given by the divine Teacher.

The student of physiology should be taught that the object of study is not merely to gain a knowledge of facts and principles. This alone will prove of little benefit. We may understand the importance of ventilation, our room may be supplied with pure air, but unless we fill our lungs properly we will suffer the results of poor respiration. The great requisite in teaching these principles is to impress students with their importance so that they will conscientiously put them into practice.

Let students be impressed with the thought that the body is a temple in which God desires to dwell, that it must be kept pure, the abiding place of high and noble thoughts. As they study physiology and see that they are indeed "fearfully and wonderfully made" (Ps. 139:14), they will be inspired with reverence. Instead of marring God's handiwork, they will have an ambition to make all that is possible of themselves, in order to fulfill the Creator's glorious plan. Thus they will come to regard obedience to the laws of health, not as a matter of sacrifice or self-denial, but as it really is, an inestimable privilege and blessing.

Chapter 22

Temperance
and Dietetics

Every student needs to understand the relation between plain living and high thinking. It rests with us individually to decide whether our lives shall be controlled by the mind or by the body. Each one makes the choice that shapes the life, and no pains should be spared to understand the forces with which we have to deal, and the influences that mold character and destiny.

Intemperance is an enemy against which all need to be guarded. The rapid increase of this terrible evil should arouse everyone to warfare against it. Instruction on temperance topics should be given in every school and in every home. Young people should understand the effect of alcohol, tobacco, and like poisons in breaking down the body, beclouding the mind, and sensualizing the soul. It should be made plain that those who use these things cannot long possess the full strength of their physical, mental, or moral faculties.

But in order to reach the root of intemperance we must go deeper than the use of alcohol or tobacco. Idleness, evil associations, or lack of aim, may be the predisposing cause. Often the cause is found at the home table, in families that consider themselves strictly temperate. Anything that disorders digestion, that creates undue mental excitement, or in any way enfeebles the system, disturbing the balance of the mental and physical powers, weakens the control of the mind over the body, and thus tends toward intemperance. The downfall of many a promising young person might be traced to unnatural appetites created by an unwholesome diet.

Tea and coffee, condiments, confectionery, and pastries, all are active causes of indigestion. Flesh food also is harmful. Its naturally stimulating effect should be a sufficient argument against its use, and the almost universally diseased condition of animals makes it doubly objectionable. It tends to irritate the nerves and excite the passions, thus giving the balance of power to the lower propensities.

Those who accustom themselves to a rich, stimulating diet, find after a time that the stomach is not satisfied with simple food. It demands that which is more and more highly seasoned, pungent, and stimulating. As the nerves become disordered and the system weakened, the will seems powerless to resist the unnatural craving. The delicate coating of the stomach becomes irritated and inflamed until the most stimulating food fails to give relief. A thirst is created that nothing but strong drink will quench.

It is the beginnings of evil that should be guarded against. In instructing the young, the effect of apparently small deviations from right should be made plain. Teach students the value of a simple, healthful diet in preventing the desire for unnatural stimulants. Establish the habit of self-control early in life. Impress the young with the thought that they are to be masters, not slaves. God has made them rulers of the kingdom within them, and they are to exercise their Heaven-appointed kingship. When such instruction is faithfully given, the results will extend far beyond the students themselves. Influences will reach out that will save thousands of men and women who are on the very brink of ruin.

Diet and Mental Development

The relation of diet to intellectual development should be given far more attention than it has received. Mental confusion and dullness are often the result of errors in diet.

It is frequently urged that appetite is a safe guide in the selection of food. If the laws of health had always been obeyed, that would be true. But through wrong habits, continued from generation to generation, appetite has become so perverted that it is constantly craving some hurtful gratification. As a guide it cannot now be trusted.

In the study of hygiene, students should be taught the nutrient value of different foods. The effect of a concentrated and stimulating diet, also of foods deficient in the elements of nutrition, should be made plain. Tea and coffee, fine-flour bread, pickles, coarse vegetables, candies, condiments, and pastries fail of supplying proper nutriment. Many a student has broken down as the result of using such foods. Many a puny child, incapable of vigorous effort of mind or body, is the victim of an impoverished diet. Grains, fruits, nuts, and vegetables, in proper combination, contain all the elements of nutrition. When properly prepared, they constitute the diet that best promotes both physical and mental strength.

There is need to consider not only the properties of the food but its adaptation to the eater. Often food that can be eaten freely by persons engaged in physical labor must be avoided by those whose work is chiefly mental. Attention should be given also to the proper combination of foods. By brain workers and others of sedentary pursuits, only a few kinds of food should be taken at a meal.

Overeating, even of the most wholesome food, is to be guarded against. Nature can use no more than is required for building up the various organs of the body, and excess clogs the system. Many a student is supposed to have broken down from overstudy, when the real cause was overeating. If proper attention is given to the laws of health, there is little danger from mental taxation. But in many cases of so-called mental failure it is the overcrowding of the stomach that wearies the body and weakens the mind.

In most cases two meals a day are preferable to three. Supper, when taken at an early hour, interferes with the digestion of the previous meal. When taken later, it is not itself digested before bedtime. Thus the stomach does not secure proper rest. The sleep is disturbed, the brain and nerves are wearied, and the appetite for breakfast is impaired. The whole system is unrefreshed and unready for the day's duties.

The importance of regularity in the time for eating and sleeping should not be overlooked. Since the work of building up the body takes place during the hours of rest, it is essential, especially when one is young, that sleep should be regular and abundant.

So far as possible we should avoid hurried eating. The shorter the time for a meal, the less should be eaten. It is better to omit a meal than to eat without proper mastication.

Mealtime should be a relaxing and social occasion. Everything that can burden or irritate should be avoided. Let trust and kindliness and gratitude to the Giver of all good be cherished, and the conversation will be cheerful, a pleasant flow of thought that will uplift without wearying.

The observance of temperance and regularity in all things has a wonderful power. It will do more than circumstances or natural endowments to promote that sweetness and serenity of disposition which count so much in smoothing life's pathway. At the same time the power of self-control thus acquired will be most valuable for grappling successfully with the stern duties and realities that await every human being.

Wisdom's "ways are ways of pleasantness, and all her paths are peace." Prov. 3:17. Let every young man and woman in our land, with the possibilities before them of a destiny higher than that of crowned kings, ponder the lesson conveyed in the words of the wise man, "Blessed are you, O land, when . . . your princes feast at the proper time—for strength and not for drunkenness!" Eccl. 10:17.

Chapter 23

Recreation

There is a difference between recreation and amusement. Recreation, when true to its name, re-creation, tends to strengthen and build up. It provides refreshment for mind and body, and thus enables us to return with new vigor to the earnest work of life. Amusement, on the other hand, is pursued for the sake of pleasure and is often carried to excess. It absorbs the energies that are required for useful work and thus proves a hindrance to life's true success.

The whole body is designed for action, and unless the physical powers are kept in health by active exercise, the mental powers cannot long be used to their highest capacity. The physical inaction that seems almost inevitable in the schoolroom—together with other unhealthful conditions—makes it a trying place for children, especially for those of feeble constitution. Often the ventilation is insufficient. Ill-formed seats encourage unnatural positions, thus cramping the action of the lungs and the heart. Here little children have to spend from three to five hours a day, breathing air that may be infected with the germs of disease. No wonder that in the schoolroom the foundation of lifelong illness often is laid.

The brain, the most delicate of all the physical organs, and from which the nervous energy of the whole system is derived, suffers the greatest injury. By being forced into premature or excessive activity, and this under unhealthful conditions, it is enfeebled, and often the evil results are permanent.

Children should not be long confined indoors, nor should they be required to apply themselves closely to study until a good foundation has been laid for physical development. For the first eight or ten years of a child's life the field or garden is the best schoolroom, the mother the best teacher, nature the best lesson book. Even when children are old enough to attend school, their health should be regarded as of greater importance than a knowledge of books. They should be surrounded with the conditions most favorable to both physical and mental growth.

Children are not the only ones endangered by lack of air and exercise. In the higher as well as the lower schools these essentials to health are still too often neglected. Many students sit day after day in a poorly ventilated room bending over their books, their chest so contracted that they cannot take a full, deep breath. Their blood moves sluggishly, their feet cold, their head hot. The body not being sufficiently nourished, the muscles are weakened, and the whole system is enervated and diseased. Often such students become lifelong invalids. If they had pursued their studies under proper conditions, with regular exercise in the sunlight and open air, they might have come from school with increased physical as well as mental strength.

Exercise Has Value

Students who with limited time and means are struggling to gain an education should realize that time spent in physical exercise is not lost. Those who continually pore over their books will find, after a time, that the mind has lost its freshness. Those who give proper attention to physical development will make greater advancement in literary lines than they would if they devoted their entire time to study.

Physical inaction lessens not only mental but moral power. The brain nerves that connect with the whole system are the medium through which Heaven communicates with humans, and affects the inmost life. Whatever hinders the circulation of the electric current in the nervous system, thus weakening the vital powers and lessening mental susceptibility, makes it more difficult to arouse the moral nature.

Again, excessive study, by increasing the flow of blood to the brain, creates morbid excitability that tends to lessen the power of self-control. Thus the door is opened to impurity. The misuse or nonuse of the physical powers is largely responsible for the tide of corruption that is overspreading the world. "Pride, fullness of bread, and abundance of idleness" are as deadly foes to human progress in this generation as when they led to the destruction of Sodom.

Teachers should understand these things, and should instruct their pupils in these lines. Teach the students that right living depends on right thinking, and that physical activity is essential to purity of thought.

Concern About Athletics

The question of suitable recreation is one that teachers often find perplexing. Gymnastic exercises fill a useful place in many schools, but without careful supervision they are often carried to excess. Many youth, by their attempted feats of strength, have done themselves lifelong injury.

Exercise in a gymnasium, however well conducted, cannot supply the place of recreation in the open air, and for this our schools should afford better opportunity. Vigorous exercise the students must have, yet teachers are troubled as they consider the influence of athletic sports both on the students' progress in school and on their success in afterlife. The games that occupy so much of their time are diverting the mind from study. They are not helping to prepare the young for practical, earnest work in life. Their influence does not tend toward refinement or generosity.

Some of the most popular amusements, such as football and boxing, have become schools of brutality. They are developing the same characteristics as did the games of ancient Rome. The love of domination, the pride in mere brute force, the reckless disregard of life, are exerting on young people a power to demoralize that is appalling.

Other athletic games, though not so brutalizing, are scarcely less objectionable because of the excess to which they are carried. They stimulate the love of pleasure and excitement, thus fostering a distaste for useful labor, a disposition to shun practical duties and responsibilities.

They tend to destroy a relish for life's sober realities and tranquil enjoyments. Thus the door is opened to dissipation and lawlessness, with terrible results.

As ordinarily conducted, parties of pleasure also are a hindrance to real growth of mind or character. Frivolous associations, habits of extravagance, of pleasure seeking, and too often of dissipation, are formed that shape the whole life for evil. In place of such amusements, parents and teachers can do much to supply wholesome and life-giving diversions.

In this, as in everything else that concerns our well-being, Inspiration has pointed the way. In early ages, life was simple for the people who were under God's direction,. They lived close to the heart of nature. Children shared in the work of their parents and studied the beauties and mysteries of nature's treasure house. And in the quiet of field and wood they pondered those mighty truths handed down as a sacred trust from generation to generation. Such training produced strong men and women.

In this age, life has become artificial, and people have degenerated. While we may not return fully to the simple habits of those early times, we may learn from them lessons that will make our seasons of recreation what the name implies—seasons of true upbuilding for body, mind, and soul.

The surroundings of the home and the school are closely related to the question of recreation. In the choice of a home or the location of a school, the surroundings should be considered. Parents with whom the mental and physical well-being of their children is of greater moment than money or the claims and customs of society, should endeavor to provide for their children the benefit of nature's teaching, and recreation amidst her surroundings. It would be a great aid in educational work if every school could be so situated as to afford the students land for cultivation, and access to the fields and woods.

In lines of recreation for the student the best results will be attained through the personal cooperation of the teacher. True teachers can impart to their students few gifts so valuable as the gift of their own companionship. It is true of men and women, and how much more of young people and children, that only as we come in touch through sympathy can we understand them; and we need to understand in order to benefit most effectively. To strengthen the tie of sympathy between teachers and students, few things count so much as pleasant association together outside the schoolroom. In some schools the teachers are always with their pupils in their hours of recreation. It would be well for our schools were this practice followed more generally. The sacrifice demanded would be great but teachers would reap a rich reward.

No recreation will prove so great a blessing to the children and youth as that which makes them helpful to others. Naturally enthusiastic and impressible, the young are quick to respond to suggestion. In planning for the culture of plants, let the teacher seek to awaken an interest in beautifying the school grounds and the schoolroom. A double benefit will result. That which the students seek to beautify they will be unwilling to have marred or defaced. A refined taste, a love of order, and a habit of care-taking will be encouraged. The spirit of fellowship and cooperation that is developed will be a lifelong blessing.

A new interest may also be given to the work of the garden or the excursion in field or wood by encouraging students to remember those shut in from these pleasant places, and to share with them the beautiful things of nature.

The watchful teacher will find many opportunities for directing students to acts of helpfulness. By little children, especially, the teacher is regarded with almost unbounded confidence and respect. Whatever he or she may suggest as to ways of helping in the home, faithfulness in the daily tasks, ministry to the sick or poor, can hardly fail to bring forth fruit. And thus again a double gain will be secured. The kindly suggestion will react upon its author. Gratitude and cooperation on the part of parents will lighten the burden of teachers and brighten their paths.

Attention to recreation and physical culture will no doubt at times interrupt the regular routine of schoolwork, but the interruption will prove no real hindrance. In the invigoration of mind and body, the fostering of an unselfish spirit, and the binding together of pupil and teacher by ties of common interest and friendly association, the expenditure of time and effort will be repaid a hundredfold. A worthwhile outlet will be afforded for that restless energy which is so often a source of danger to the young. As a safeguard against evil, the preoccupation of the mind with good is worth more than unnumbered barriers of law and discipline.

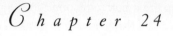

Manual Training

At the Creation, work was appointed as a blessing. It meant development, power, happiness. The changed condition of the earth through the curse of sin has brought a change in the conditions of work, yet though now attended with anxiety, weariness, and pain, it is still a source of happiness and development. And it is a safeguard against temptation. Its discipline places a check on self-indulgence, and promotes industry, purity, and firmness. Thus it becomes a part of God's great plan for our recovery from the Fall.

Young people should be led to see the true dignity of work. God is a constant worker. All things in nature do their allotted work. Action pervades the whole creation, and in order to fulfill our mission we, too, must be active.

We are workers together with God. He gives us the earth and its treasures, but we must adapt them to our use and comfort. He causes the trees to grow, but we prepare the timber and build the house. He has hidden in the earth the gold and silver, the iron and coal, but only through work can we obtain them.

We should show young people that while God has created and constantly controls all things, He has endowed us with a power not wholly unlike His. To us has been given a degree of control over the forces of nature. As God called forth the earth in its beauty out of chaos, so we can bring order and beauty out of confusion. And though all things are now marred with evil, in our completed work we feel a joy similar to His, when, looking on the fair earth, He pronounced it "very good."

As a rule, the exercise most beneficial to young people will be found in useful work. Little children find both diversion and development in play, and their sports should be such as to promote not only physical but mental and spiritual growth. As they gain strength and intelligence, the best recreation will be found in some line of useful activity. That which trains the hand to helpfulness and teaches young people to bear their share of life's burdens, is most effective in promoting growth of mind and character.

Young people need to be taught that life means earnest work, responsibility, care-taking. They need a training that will make them practical men and women who can cope with emergencies. They should be taught that the discipline of systematic, well-regulated labor is essential not only as a safeguard against the vicissitudes of life but as an aid to all-around development.

Notwithstanding all that has been said and written concerning the dignity of physical work, the feeling prevails that it is degrading. Young men want to become teachers, clerks, merchants, physicians, lawyers, or to occupy some other position that does not require physical effort. Young women shun housework and seek an education in other lines. These need to learn that no man or woman is degraded by honest toil. That which degrades is idleness and selfish dependence. Idleness fosters self-indulgence, and the result is a life empty and barren—a field inviting the growth of every evil. "The earth which drinks in the rain that often comes upon it, and bears herbs useful for those by whom it is cultivated, receives blessing from God; but if it bears thorns and briers, it is rejected, and is near to being cursed, whose end is to be burned." Heb. 6:7, 8.

Many branches of study that consume the student's time are not essential to usefulness or happiness, but every young person should have a thorough acquaintance with everyday duties. If need be, a young woman can dispense with a knowledge of a foreign language and algebra, or even of the piano, but it is indispensable that she learn to perform efficiently the duties that pertain to homemaking. In many ways, life's happiness is bound up with faithfulness in common duties.

Since both men and women have a part in home-making, boys as well as girls should gain a knowledge of household duties. To make a bed and put a room in order, to wash dishes, to prepare a meal, to wash and repair his own clothing, is a training that need not make any boy less manly; it will make him happier and more useful. And if girls, in turn, could learn to use the saw and the hammer, as well as the rake and hoe, they would be better fitted to meet the emergencies of life.

God Honors Workers

Children and youth should learn from the Bible how God has honored the work of the everyday toiler. Let them read of "the sons of the prophets" (2 Kings 6:1-7), students at school who were building a house and for whom God performed a miracle to save a borrowed ax. Let them read of Jesus the carpenter, and Paul the tentmaker, who linked the toil of the craftsman with the highest ministry, human and divine. Let them read about the boy whose five loaves were used by the Savior in that wonderful miracle for the feeding of the multitude; of Dorcas the seamstress, called back from death that she might continue to make garments for the poor; of the wise woman described in Proverbs, who "seeks wool and flax, and willingly works with her hands," who "provides food for her household, and a portion for her maidservants," who "plants a vineyard" and "strengthens her arms," who "extends her hand to the poor, yes, . . . reaches out her hands to the needy," who "watches over the ways of her household, and does not eat the bread of idleness." Prov. 31:13, 15; 31:16, 17, 20, 27.

Of such a person, God says: "She shall be praised. Give her of the fruit of her hands, and let her own works praise her in the gates." Prov. 31:30, 31.

For every child the first school for training in industries should be the home. And, so far as possible, facilities for manual training should be connected with every school. To a great degree such training would supply the place of the gymnasium, with the additional benefit of affording valuable discipline.

Manual training deserves far more attention than it has received. Schools should be established that, in addition to the highest mental and moral culture, shall provide the best possible facilities for physical development and practical industries. Instruction should be given in many of the most useful trades, as well as in household economy, healthful cooking, sewing, dressmaking, treatment of the sick, and similar lines. Gardens, workshops, and treatment rooms should be provided, and the work in every line should be under the direction of skilled instructors.

The work should be thorough and have a definite aim. While every person needs some knowledge of various handicrafts, all should become proficient in at least one. All young people, on leaving school, should have a knowledge of some trade or occupation by which, if need be, they may earn a livelihood.

The objection most often urged against industrial training in school is the large outlay and heavy expense involved. But the object to be gained is worthy of its cost. No other work committed to us is so important as the training of our youth, and every outlay demanded for its right accomplishment is money well spent.

Even from the viewpoint of financial results, the outlay required for manual training would prove the truest economy. The expenditure for gardens, workshops, and facilities for water treatments would be more than met by the saving on hospitals and reformatories. And the youth themselves, trained to habits of industry, and skilled in lines of useful and productive labor—who can estimate their value to society and to the nation!

As a relaxation from study, occupations pursued in the open air and affording exercise for the whole body, are the most beneficial. No line of manual training is of more value than agriculture. The Bible says much about agriculture—that it was God's plan for human beings to till the earth, that the first man, the ruler of the whole world, was given a garden to cultivate. Many of the world's greatest people, its real nobility, have worked the soil. Of those who cultivate the soil the Bible declares, "They are well instructed; their God teaches them" Isa. 28:26, NRSV. And again, "Whoever keeps the fig tree will eat its fruit." Prov. 27:18.

In the study of agriculture, let students be given not only theory, but practice. While they learn what science can teach in regard to the nature and preparation of the soil, the value of different crops, and the best methods of production, let them put their knowledge to use. Teachers should share the work with their students, and show what results can be achieved through skillful, intelligent effort. Thus may be awakened a genuine interest, an ambition to do the work in the best possible manner. Such an ambition, together with the invigorating effect of exercise, sunshine, and pure air, will create a love for agricultural work that with many youth will determine their choice of an occupation.

Manual Training Needed by Professionals

The benefit of manual training is needed also by professional people. They may have brilliant minds; they may be quick to catch ideas; their knowledge and skill may secure for them admission to their chosen calling; yet they may still be far from possessing a fitness for its duties. An education derived chiefly from books leads to superficial thinking. Practical work encourages close observation and independent thought. Rightly performed, it tends to develop that practical wisdom which we call common sense. It develops ability to plan and execute, strengthens courage and perseverance, and calls for the exercise of tact and skill.

Physicians who have laid a foundation for their professional knowledge by actual service in the sickroom will have a quickness of insight, an all-around knowledge, and an ability in emergencies to render needed service—all essential qualifications that only a practical training can so fully impart.

Ministers, missionaries, and teachers will find their influence with the people greatly increased when it is demonstrated that they possess the knowledge and skill required for the practical duties of everyday life.

In acquiring an education, many students would gain a most valuable training if they would become self-sustaining. Instead of incurring debts or depending on the self-denial of their parents, let young men and young women depend on themselves. They will thus learn the value of money, the value of time, strength, and opportunities, and will be under far less temptation to indulge idle and spendthrift habits. The lessons of economy, industry, self-denial, practical business management, and steadfastness of purpose, thus mastered, would prove a most important part of their equipment for the battle of life.

Let young people be impressed with the thought that education is not to teach them how to escape life's disagreeable tasks and heavy burdens; its purpose is to lighten the work by teaching better methods and higher aims. Teach them that life's true aim is not to secure the greatest possible gain for themselves, it is to honor their Maker in doing their part of the world's work and lending a helpful hand to those weaker or more ignorant.

One great reason why physical work is looked down on is the slipshod, unthinking way in which it is often performed. It is done from necessity, not from choice. The worker puts no heart into it, and he neither preserves self-respect nor wins the respect of others. Manual training should correct this error. It should develop habits of accuracy and thoroughness. Students should learn tact and system. They should learn to economize time and make every move count. They should not only be taught the best methods, they should be inspired with ambition constantly to improve.

Such training will make the youth masters and not slaves of work. It will lighten the lot of the hard toiler, and will ennoble even the humblest occupation. Those who regard work as mere drudgery, and settle down to it with self-complacent ignorance, making no effort to improve, will find it indeed a burden. But those who recognize science in the humblest work will see in it nobility and beauty, and will take pleasure in performing it with faithfulness and efficiency.

C h a p t e r 25

Education and Character

True education does not ignore the value of scientific knowledge or literary acquirements, but above information it values power; above power, goodness; above intellectual acquirements, character. The world does not so much need men and women of great intellect as of noble character. It needs people in whom ability is controlled by steadfast principle.

"Wisdom is the principal thing; therefore get wisdom." "The tongue of the wise uses knowledge rightly." Prov. 4:7; 15:2. True education imparts this wisdom. It teaches the best use not merely of one but of all our powers and acquirements. Thus it covers the whole circle of obligation—to ourselves, to the world, and to God.

Character building is the most important work ever entrusted to human beings, and never was its diligent study so important as now. Never was any previous generation called to meet issues so momentous. Never were young men and women confronted by perils so great as confront them today.

At this critical time, what is the trend of the education given? What motive is appealed to most often? Self-seeking. Much of today's education is a perversion of the name. True education provides a counter influence to the selfish ambition, greed for power, and disregard for the rights and needs of humanity that are the curse of our world.

No Place for Selfish Rivalry

God's plan of life has a place for every human being. All are to improve their talents to the utmost, and faithfulness in doing this, whether the gifts be few or many, entitles them to honor. In God's plan there is no place for selfish rivalry. Those who measure themselves by themselves, and compare themselves among themselves, are not wise. 2 Cor. 10:12. Whatever we do is to be done "heartily, as to the Lord . . . knowing that from the Lord you will receive the reward of the inheritance; for you serve the Lord Christ." Col. 3:23, 24. But how different is much of the education now given! From the child's earliest years it is an appeal to emulation and rivalry; it fosters selfishness, the root of all evil.

Thus is created strife for supremacy, and the system of "cramming" is encouraged that in some cases destroys health and unfits for usefulness. In many others, emulation leads to dishonesty, and by fostering ambition and discontent, it embitters the life and helps fill the world with restless, turbulent people who are a continual menace to society. Nor does danger pertain to methods only. It is found also in the subject matter of the studies.

In the study of language and literature, from what fountains are the youth taught to drink? From the wells of paganism, from springs fed by the corruptions of ancient heathendom. They are assigned to study authors who, it is clear, have no regard for the principles of morality.

And of how many modern authors also might the same be said! With how many do the grace and beauty of language merely disguise principles that in their real deformity would repel the reader!

Besides these there is a multitude of fiction writers, luring to pleasant dreams in palaces of ease. These writers may not be open to the charge of immorality, yet their work is no less productive of evil. It is robbing thousands and thousands of the time, energy, and self-discipline demanded by the stern problems of life.

In the study of science, as generally pursued, there are dangers equally great. Evolution and its kindred errors are taught in schools of every grade, from kindergarten to college. Thus the study of science, which should impart a knowledge of God, is so mingled with human speculations and theories that it tends to infidelity.

Even Bible study, as too often conducted in the schools, is robbing the world of the priceless treasure of the Word of God. The work of "higher criticism" in dissecting, conjecturing, reconstructing, is destroying faith in the Bible as a divine revelation. It is robbing God's Word of power to control, uplift, and inspire human lives.

Contact With False Teachings

As young people go out into the world to encounter its allurements to sin—the passion for money getting, for amusement and indulgence, for display, luxury, and extravagance, the overreaching, fraud, robbery, and ruin—what are the teachings to be met there?

Spiritualism asserts that human beings are unfallen demigods, that "each mind will judge itself," "all sins committed are innocent," for "whatever is, is right," and "God does not condemn." The basest of human beings are represented as in heaven, and highly exalted there. Thus it teaches that "It matters not what you do; live as you please, heaven is your home." Multitudes are thus led to believe that desire is the highest law, that license is liberty, and that the members of the human race are accountable only to themselves.

With such teaching given at the very outset of life, when impulse is strongest and the demand for self-restraint and purity is most urgent, where are the safeguards of virtue? What is to prevent the world from becoming a second Sodom?

At the same time rebellious spirits are seeking to sweep away all law, both divine and human. The centralizing of wealth and power; the vast combinations for enriching the few at the expense of the many; the combinations of the poorer classes for the defense of their interests and claims; the spirit of unrest, of riot and bloodshed—all are tending to involve the whole world in a struggle similar to that which convulsed France in the eighteenth century.

Such are the influences to be met by young people today. To stand amidst such upheavals they must now lay the foundations of character.

In every generation and in every land the true foundation and pattern for character building have been the same. The divine law, "You shall love the Lord your God with all your heart; . . . and your neighbor as yourself" (Luke 10:27)—the great principle made manifest in the character and life of our Savior—is the only secure foundation, the only sure guide.

"Wisdom and knowledge will be the stability of your times" (Isa.

33:6, Leeser's translation)—that wisdom and knowledge which God's Word alone can impart.

Here is the only safeguard for individual integrity, for the purity of the home, the well-being of society, or the stability of the nation. Amidst all life's perplexities, dangers, and conflicting claims, the one safe and sure rule is to do what God says. "The precepts of the Lord are right," and "those who do these things shall never be moved." Ps. 19:8; 15:5, NRSV.

C h a p t e r   26

Methods
of Teaching

For centuries education has had to do chiefly with the memory. This faculty of the mind has been taxed to the utmost, while the other mental powers have not been correspondingly developed. Students have spent their time crowding the mind with knowledge, very little of which could be utilized. The mind thus burdened with that which it cannot digest and assimilate is weakened; it becomes incapable of vigorous, self-reliant effort, and is content to depend on the judgment and perception of others.

Seeing the evils of this method, some have gone to another extreme. In their view, people need only to develop that which is within them. Such education leads students to self-sufficiency, thus cutting them off from the source of true knowledge and power.

The education that consists in the training of the memory tends to discourage independent thought, and has a moral bearing that is too little appreciated. As students sacrifice the power to reason and judge for themselves, they become incapable of discriminating between truth and error, and fall an easy prey to deception. They are easily led to follow tradition and custom.

It is a fact widely ignored, though never without danger, that error rarely appears for what it really is. It is by mingling with or attaching itself to truth that it gains acceptance. The eating of the tree of knowledge of good and evil caused the ruin of our first parents, and the acceptance of a mingling of good and evil is the ruin of men and women today. The mind that depends on the judgment of others is certain, sooner or later, to be misled.

Only through individual dependence upon God can we possess the power to discriminate between right and wrong. Each person is to learn from Him through His Word. Our reasoning powers were given us to use, and God desires them to be exercised. "Come now, and let us reason together" (Isa. 1:18), He invites us. In reliance upon Him we may have wisdom to "refuse the evil and choose the good." Isa. 7:15; James 1:5.

Personal Element Essential

In all true teaching the personal element is essential. Christ in His teaching dealt with people individually. By personal contact and association He trained the Twelve. In private, often to but one listener, He gave His most precious instruction. He opened His richest treasures to the honored rabbi at the night conference on the Mount of Olives, and to the despised woman at the well of Sychar, for in these hearers He discerned the impressible heart, the open mind, the receptive spirit. Even the crowd that so often thronged His steps was not to Christ an indiscriminate mass of human beings. He spoke directly to every mind and appealed to every heart. He watched the faces of His hearers, marked the lighting up of the countenance, the quick, responsive glance, which told that truth had reached the soul; and there vibrated in His heart the answering chord of sympathetic joy.

Christ discerned possibilities in every human being. He was not turned aside by an unpromising exterior or by unfavorable surroundings. He called Matthew from the tollbooth, and Peter and his associates from the fishing boat, to learn of Him.

The same personal interest, the same attention to individual development, are needed in educational work today. Many apparently unpromising young people are richly endowed with talents that are not being used. Their faculties lie hidden because of a lack of discernment on the part of their teachers. In many a boy or girl outwardly as unattractive as a rough-hewn stone may be found precious material that will stand the test of heat, storm, and pressure. True educators, keeping in view what their students may become, will recognize the value of the material with which they are working. They will take a personal interest in each pupil and will seek to develop all their powers. However imperfect, every effort to conform to right principles will be encouraged.

Every young person should be taught the necessity and the power of application. On this, far more than on genius or talent, success depends. Without application the most brilliant talents avail little, while with rightly directed effort persons of very ordinary natural abilities have accomplished wonders. And genius, at whose achievements we marvel, is almost invariably united with untiring, concentrated effort.

All the Faculties to Be Developed

Young people should be taught to aim at the development of all their faculties, the weaker as well as the stronger. With many there is a disposition to restrict their study to certain lines for which they have a natural liking. This error should be guarded against. The natural aptitudes indicate the direction of the lifework, and, when legitimate, should be carefully cultivated. At the same time it must be kept in mind that a well-balanced character and efficient work in any line depend, to a great degree, on that symmetrical development which is the result of thorough, all-around training.

Teachers should constantly aim at simplicity and effectiveness. They should teach largely by illustration, and even in dealing with older pupils should be careful to make every explanation plain and clear. Many students well advanced in years are but children in understanding.

An important element in educational work is enthusiasm. On this point there is a useful suggestion in a remark once made by a celebrated actor. The archbishop of Canterbury asked him why actors in a play affect their audiences so powerfully while ministers of the gospel often affect theirs so little. "With due submission to your grace," replied the actor, "permit me to say that the reason is plain: It lies in the power of enthusiasm. We on the stage speak of things imaginary as if they were real, and you in the pulpit speak of things real as if they were imaginary."

Teachers are dealing with things real, and they should speak of them with all the force and enthusiasm that a knowledge of their reality and importance can inspire.

Teachers should see to it that their work tends to definite results. Before attempting to teach a subject, they should have a distinct plan in mind, and should know just what they want to accomplish. They should not rest satisfied with the presentation of any subject until their students understand the principle involved, perceive its truth, and are able to state clearly what they have learned.

So long as the great purpose of education is kept in view, students should be encouraged to advance just as far as their capabilities will permit. But before taking up the higher branches of study, let them master the lower. This is too often neglected. Even among students in the higher schools and the colleges there is great deficiency in knowledge of the common branches of education. Many students devote their time to higher mathematics when they are incapable of keeping simple accounts. Many study elocution with a view to acquiring the graces of oratory when they are unable to read in an intelligible and impressive manner. Many who have finished the study of rhetoric fail in the composition and spelling of an ordinary letter.

A thorough knowledge of the essentials of education should be not only the condition of admission to a higher course, but the constant test for continuance and advancement.

The Study and Use of Language

In every branch of education there are objects to be gained more important than those secured by mere technical knowledge. Take language, for example. More important than the acquirement of foreign languages, living or dead, is the ability to write and speak one's mother tongue with ease and accuracy. But no training gained through a knowledge of grammatical rules can compare in importance with the study of language from a higher point of view. With this study, to a great degree, is bound up life's happiness or sorrow, prosperity or adversity.

The chief requisite of language is that it be pure and kind and true—"the outward expression of an inward grace." God says: "Whatever things are true, whatever things are noble, whatever things are just, whatever things are pure, whatever things are lovely, whatever things are of good report, if there is any virtue and if there is anything praiseworthy—meditate on these things." Phil. 4:8. And if such are the thoughts, such will be the oral expression.

The best school for this language study is the home, but since the work of the home is often neglected, it devolves on teachers to aid their pupils in forming right habits of speech.

Teachers can do much to discourage the evil habit of backbiting, gossip, and ungenerous criticism that is the curse of the community, the neighborhood, and the home. No pains should be spared to impress upon students the fact that this habit reveals a lack of culture, refinement, and true goodness of heart. It unfits a person both for the society of the truly cultured and refined in this world and for association with the holy ones of heaven.

We think with horror of the cannibal who feasts on the still warm flesh of his victim, but are the results of this practice more terrible than the agony and ruin caused by misrepresenting motive, blackening reputation, dissecting character? The young should be taught what God says about these things: "Death and life are in the power of the tongue." Prov. 18:21. Backbiters are classed with "haters of God," with "inventors of evil things," with those who are "violent, proud, boasters," "full of envy, murder, strife, deceit, evil-mindedness." Rom. 1:30, 31, 29. People whom God accounts as citizens of Zion are those "who speak the truth from their heart; who do not slander with their tongue, . . . nor take up a reproach against their neighbors." Ps. 15:2, 3, NRSV.

God's Word condemns also the use of meaningless phrases and expletives that border on profanity. It condemns deceptive compliments, evasions of truth, exaggerations, and misrepresentations in trade, that are current in society and in the business world. "Let your 'Yes' be, 'Yes,' and your 'No,' 'No.' For whatever is more than these is from the evil one." Matt. 5:37. "Like a maniac who shoots deadly firebrands and arrows, so is one who deceives a neighbor and says 'I am only joking!'" Prov. 26:18, 19, NRSV.

Closely allied to gossip is the covert insinuation, the sly innuendo, by which the unclean in heart imply the evil they dare not openly express. Teach young people to shun like leprosy every approach to these practices.

In the use of language there is perhaps no fault that old and young are more ready to pass over lightly in themselves than hasty, impatient speech. They think it a sufficient excuse to plead, "I was off my guard, and did not really mean what I said." But God's Word does not treat it lightly. The Scripture says: "Do you see someone who is hasty in speech? There is more hope for a fool than for anyone like that." "Like a city breached, without walls, is one who lacks self-control." Prov. 29:20; 25:28, NRSV.

In one moment, the hasty, passionate, careless tongue may produce evil that a whole lifetime's repentance cannot undo. Oh, the hearts that are broken, the friends estranged, the lives wrecked, by the harsh, hasty words of those who might have brought help and healing!

The Grace of Self-forgetfulness

One characteristic that should be especially cherished and cultivated in every child is self-forgetfulness, a characteristic that imparts unconscious grace to the life. Of all excellent traits of character this is one of the most beautiful, and for every true lifework it is one of the qualifications most essential.

Children need appreciation, sympathy, and encouragement, but care should be taken not to foster in them a love of praise. It is not wise to give them special notice, or to repeat before them their clever sayings. Parents and teachers who keep in view the true ideal of character and the possibilities of achievement, cannot cherish or encourage self-sufficiency. They will not encourage in youth the desire or effort to display their ability or proficiency. Every person who looks higher than himself or herself will be humble, yet will possess a dignity that is not abashed or disconcerted by outward display or human greatness.

It is not by arbitrary law or rule that the graces of character are developed. It is by dwelling in the atmosphere of the pure, the noble, the true. And wherever there is purity of heart and nobleness of character, it will be revealed in purity and nobleness of action and of speech.

"Those who love a pure heart and are gracious in speech will have the King as a friend." Prov. 22:11, NRSV.

Study of History Builds Character

As with language, so with every other study; it may be conducted so that it will tend to strengthen and upbuild character. Of no study is this truer than of history. Let it be considered from the divine point of view.

As too often taught, history is little more than a record of the rise and fall of kings, the intrigues of courts, the victories and defeats of armies— a story of ambition and greed, of deception, cruelty, and bloodshed. Thus taught, its results cannot but be detrimental. The heart-sickening reiteration of crimes and atrocities, the enormities, the cruelties portrayed, plant seeds that in many lives bring forth fruit in a harvest of evil.

It is far better to learn, in the light of God's Word, the causes that govern the rise and fall of kingdoms. Teach the young to study these records and see how the true prosperity of nations has been bound up with an acceptance of divine principles. Let them study the history of great reformatory movements, and see how often these principles—though hated and their advocates sent to the dungeon and the scaffold—triumphed through these very sacrifices.

Such study will give broad, comprehensive views of life. It will help young people understand something of its relations and dependencies, how wonderfully we are bound together in the great family of society and nations, and to how great an extent the oppression or degradation of one member means a loss to all.

In the study of arithmetic and mathematics the work should be made practical. Children and youth should be taught not merely to solve imaginary problems but to keep an accurate account of their own income and outgo. Let them learn the right use of money by using it. Boys and girls should learn to select and buy their own clothing, their books, and other necessities, and by keeping an account of their expenses they will learn, as they could learn in no other way, the value and use of money. Rightly directed it will encourage habits of benevolence. It will aid the youth in learning to give, not from the mere impulse of the moment, as their feelings are stirred, but regularly and systematically.

In this way every study may become an aid in the solution of that greatest of all problems, the training of men and women for the best discharge of life's responsibilities.

Chapter 27

Deportment

The value of courtesy is too little appreciated. Many who are kind at heart lack kindliness of manner. Many who command respect by their sincerity and uprightness are sadly deficient in geniality. This lack mars their own happiness and detracts from their service to others.

Cheerfulness and courtesy should be cultivated especially by parents and teachers. All may possess a cheerful countenance, a gentle voice, a courteous manner, and these are elements of power. Children are attracted by a cheerful attitude. Show them kindness and courtesy, and they will manifest the same spirit toward you and toward one another.

True courtesy is not learned by the mere practice of rules of etiquette. Propriety of deportment is at all times to be observed. Wherever principle is not compromised, consideration of others will lead to compliance with accepted customs. But true courtesy requires no sacrifice of principle to conventionality. It ignores caste. It teaches self-respect, respect for the dignity of personhood, a regard for every member of the great human family.

There is danger of placing too high a value on mere manner and form, and devoting too much time to education in these lines. The life of strenuous effort demanded of every young person, the hard, often uncongenial work required even for life's ordinary duties, and much more for lightening the world's heavy burden of ignorance and wretchedness—these give little place for conventionalities.

Many who lay great emphasis on etiquette show little respect for anything, however excellent, that fails to meet their artificial standard. This is false education. It fosters critical pride and narrow exclusiveness.

The essence of true politeness is consideration for others. The essential, enduring education is that which broadens the sympathies and encourages universal kindliness. That so-called culture which does not make young people deferential toward their parents, appreciative of their excellences, forbearing toward their defects, and helpful to their necessities; which does not make them considerate and tender, generous and helpful toward the young, the old, and the unfortunate, and courteous toward all, is a failure.

Divinely Taught Courtesy

Real refinement of thought and manner is better learned in the school of the divine Teacher than by any observance of set rules. His love pervading the heart gives to the character those refining touches that fashion it in the semblance of His own. This education imparts a heaven-born dignity and sense of propriety. It gives a sweetness of disposition and a gentleness of manner that can never be equaled by the superficial polish of fashionable society.

The Bible enjoins courtesy, and it presents many illustrations of the unselfish spirit, the gentle grace, the winsome temper, that characterize true politeness. These are but reflections of the character of Christ. All the real tenderness and courtesy in the world, even among those who do not acknowledge His name, is from Him. And He desires these characteristics to be perfectly reflected in His children. It is His purpose that in us the world shall behold His beauty.

The most valuable treatise on etiquette ever penned is the instruction given by the Savior through the apostle Paul—words that should be ineffaceably written in the memory of every human being, young or old: "As I have loved you, that you also love one another." John 13:34.

"Love suffers long and is kind;
Love does not envy;
Love does not parade itself,
Is not puffed up;
Does not behave rudely,
Does not seek its own,
Is not provoked,
Thinks no evil;
Does not rejoice in iniquity,
But rejoices in the truth;
Bears all things,
Believes all things,
Hopes all things,
Endures all things.
Love never fails." 1 Cor. 13:4-8.

Reverence

Another precious grace that should be carefully cherished is reverence. True reverence for God is inspired by a sense of His infinite greatness and a realization of His presence. The heart of every child should be deeply impressed with this sense of the Unseen. The child should be taught to regard the hour and place of prayer and the services of public worship as sacred, because God is there. As reverence is manifested in attitude and demeanor, the feeling that inspires it will be deepened.

Young and old should study, ponder, and often repeat those words of Holy Writ that show how the place marked by God's special presence should be regarded. "Take your sandals off your feet," He commanded Moses at the burning bush, "for the place where you stand is holy ground." Exod. 3:5.

Jacob, after seeing the vision of the angels, exclaimed, "The Lord is in this place; and I did not know it. . . . This is none other than the house of God, and this is the gate of heaven!" Gen. 28:16, 17.

"The Lord is in His holy temple. Let all the earth keep silence before Him." Hab. 2:20.

"The Lord is the great God,

And the great King above all gods. . . .
Oh come, let us worship and bow down;
Let us kneel before the Lord our Maker."
. Ps. 95:3-6.

Reverence should be shown also for the name of God. Never should that name be spoken lightly or thoughtlessly. Even in prayer its frequent or needless repetition should be avoided. "Holy and awesome is His name." Ps. 111:9. Angels, as they speak it, veil their faces. With what reverence should we who are fallen and sinful take it on our lips!

We should reverence God's Word. For the printed volume we should show respect, never putting it to common uses, or handling it carelessly. And never should Scripture be quoted in a jest, or paraphrased to point a witty saying. "Every word of God is pure"; "like silver tried in a furnace of earth, purified seven times." Prov. 30:5; Ps. 12:6.

Above all, children should be taught that true reverence is shown by obedience. God has commanded nothing that is unessential, and there is no other way of manifesting reverence so pleasing to Him as obedience to His Word.

Reverence should be shown for God's representatives—for ministers, teachers, and parents who are called to speak and act in His stead. He is honored in the respect shown to them. And God has especially commanded that tender respect be shown toward the aged. He says, "The silver-haired head is a crown of glory, if it is found in the way of righteousness." Prov. 16:31. It tells of battles fought and victories gained, of burdens borne and temptations resisted. It tells of weary feet nearing their rest, of places soon to be vacant. Help the children to think of this, and they will smooth the path of the aged by their courtesy and respect, and will bring grace and beauty into their young lives as they heed the command to "rise before the aged, and defer to the old." Lev. 19:32, NRSV.

Fathers and mothers and teachers need to appreciate more fully the responsibility and honor that God has placed on them, in making them, to the child, the representatives of Himself. The character revealed in the contact of daily life will interpret to the child, for good or evil, those words of God:

"As a father pities his children, so the Lord pities those who fear

Him." Ps.103:13. "As one whom his mother comforts, so I will comfort you." Isa. 6:13.

Fortunate is the child in whom such words as these awaken love and gratitude and trust; the child to whom the tenderness and justice and longsuffering of father and mother and teacher interpret the love and justice and longsuffering of God; the child who by trust and submission and reverence toward his earthly protectors learns to trust and obey and reverence his God. Adults who impart to children or students such a gift have endowed them with a treasure more precious than the wealth of all the ages—a treasure as enduring as eternity.

Chapter 28

Relation of Dress to Education

No education can be complete that does not teach right principles in regard to dress. Without such teaching, the work of education is too often retarded and perverted. Love of dress and devotion to fashion are among the teacher's most formidable rivals and most effective hindrances.

Fashion rules with an iron hand. In many homes the strength, time, and attention of parents and children are absorbed in meeting its demands.

With many it matters not how becoming, or even beautiful, a garment may be; if the fashion changes, it must be remade or discarded. The members of the household are doomed to ceaseless effort. There is no time for training the children, no time for prayer or Bible study, no time for helping the little ones become acquainted with God through His works. There is no time and no money for charity. And often the home table is stinted. The food is poorly selected and hastily prepared, and the demands of nature are but partially supplied. The result is wrong habits of diet, which create disease or lead to intemperance.

The love of display produces extravagance, and in many young people kills the aspiration for a nobler life. Instead of pursuing an education, they early engage in some occupation to earn money for indulging the passion for clothes. And through this passion many young girls are beguiled to ruin.

In many a home the family resources are overtaxed. The father, unable to supply the demands of the mother and the children, is tempted to dishonesty, and dishonor and ruin are the result.

Even the day of worship is not exempt from fashion's domination. The church is made a parade ground, and the fashions are studied more than the sermon. The poor, unable to meet the demands of custom, stay away from church altogether.

At school, the girls, by unsuitable and uncomfortable clothing, are unfitted either for study or for recreation. Their minds are preoccupied, and the teacher has a difficult task to awaken their interest.

For breaking the spell of fashion, the teacher can often find no means more effective than contact with nature. Teach students to enjoy the delights found by river or lake or sea. Let them climb hills, watch the sunset glory, explore the treasures of wood and field, and learn the pleasure of cultivating plants and flowers. As they do this, the importance of following the latest styles will sink into insignificance.

Lead the young people to see that in dress, as in diet, plain living is indispensable to high thinking. Help them see the treasures in the Word of God, in the book of nature, and in the records of noble lives.

Turn their minds toward the suffering that they might relieve. Help them see that by every dollar squandered in display, the spender is deprived of means for feeding the hungry, clothing the naked, and comforting the sorrowful.

At the same time the young should be taught to recognize the lesson of nature, "He has made everything beautiful in its time." Eccl. 3:11. In dress, as in all things else, it is our privilege to honor our Creator. He desires our clothing to be not only neat and healthful, but appropriate and becoming.

Dress Reveals Character

The character of a man or woman is judged by their style of dress. A refined taste, a cultivated mind, will be revealed in the choice of simple and appropriate attire. Simplicity in dress, when united with modesty of demeanor, will go far toward surrounding a young woman with an atmosphere of sacred reserve.

Let girls be taught that the art of dressing well includes the ability to make their own clothing. This is an ambition that every girl should cherish. It will be a means of usefulness and independence.

It is right to love beauty and to desire it, but God wants us to love and to seek first the highest beauty—that which is imperishable. The choicest productions of human skill possess no beauty that can compare with that beauty of character which in His sight is of "great price."

Teach young people and even little children to choose for themselves that royal robe woven in heaven's loom—the "fine linen, clean and white" (Rev. 19:8) that all the holy ones of earth will wear. This robe, Christ's own spotless character, is freely offered to every human being. But all who receive it will receive and wear it here.

Teach children that as they open their minds to pure, loving thoughts and do loving and helpful deeds, they are clothing themselves with Christ's beautiful garment of character. This will make them beautiful and beloved here, and will hereafter be their title of admission to the palace of the King. His promise is: "They shall walk with Me in white, for they are worthy." Rev. 3:4.

Chapter 29

The
Sabbath

The value of the Sabbath as a means of education is beyond estimate. Whatever of ours God claims from us, He returns again, enriched, transfigured with His own glory. The tithe that He claimed from Israel was devoted to preserving in its glorious beauty the pattern of His temple in the heavens, the token of His presence on earth. So the portion of our time that He claims is given back to us, bearing His name and seal. "It is a sign," He says, "between Me and you; . . . that you may know that I am the Lord," because "in six days the Lord made the heavens and the earth, the sea, and all that is in them, and rested the seventh day. Therefore the Lord blessed the Sabbath day and hallowed it." Exod. 31:13; 20:11.

The Sabbath is a sign of creative and redeeming power. It points to God as the source of life and knowledge. It recalls our first parents' primeval glory, and thus witnesses to God's purpose to recreate us in His own image.

Both the Sabbath and the family were instituted in Eden, and in God's purpose they are forever linked together. On this day more than on any other it is possible for us to live the life of Eden. It was God's plan for the members of the family to be associated in work and study, in worship and recreation, the father as priest, and both father and mother as teachers and companions of their children. But sin has changed the conditions of life, and often the father hardly sees his children throughout the week. He is almost wholly deprived of opportunity for companionship or instruction. But God's love has set a limit to the demands of work. He places His merciful hand over the Sabbath. In His own day He preserves opportunity for the family to commune with Him, with nature, and with one another.

Since the Sabbath is the memorial of creative power, it is the day above all others when we should acquaint ourselves with God through His works. In the minds of children the very thought of the Sabbath should be connected with the beauty of natural things. Fortunate is the family that can go to the place of worship on Sabbath as Jesus and His disciples went to the synagogue—across the fields, along the shores of the lake, or through the groves. Blessed indeed are fathers and mothers who can teach their children God's written Word with illustrations from nature; who can gather under the trees, in the fresh, pure air, to study the Word and sing praises to the Father above.

By such associations parents may bind their children to their hearts, and thus to God, by ties that can never be broken.

As a means of intellectual training, the opportunities of the Sabbath are invaluable. The Sabbath School lesson should be learned, not by a hasty glance on Sabbath morning, but by careful study on Sabbath afternoon, with daily review or illustration during the week. Thus the lesson will become fixed in the memory, a treasure never to be wholly lost.

In listening to the sermon parents and children should note the scriptures quoted, and follow the line of thought, to repeat to one another at home. This will go far toward relieving the weariness with which children often listen to a sermon, and it will cultivate in all a habit of attention and connected thought.

Meditation on the themes thus suggested will open to students treasures of which they have never dreamed. They will prove in their own lives the reality of the experience described in the scripture: "Your words were found, and I ate them, and Your word was to me the joy and rejoicing of my heart." Jer. 15:16. "By them Your servant is warned, and in keeping them there is great reward." Ps. 19:10, 11.

Chapter 30

Faith
and Prayer

Faith is trusting God—believing that He loves us and knows best what is for our good. Thus it leads us to choose His way instead of our own. In place of our ignorance, it accepts His wisdom; in place of our weakness, His strength; in place of our sinfulness, His righteousness. Our lives are already His; faith acknowledges His ownership and accepts its blessing. Truth, uprightness, purity, have been pointed out as secrets of life's success. Faith puts us in possession of these principles.

Every good impulse or aspiration is the gift of God. Faith receives from God the life that alone can produce true growth and efficiency.

Make very plain how to exercise faith. To every promise of God there are conditions. If we are willing to do His will, all His strength is ours. Whatever gift He promises is in the promise itself. "The seed is the word of God." Luke 8:11. As surely as the oak is in the acorn, so surely is the gift of God in His promise. If we receive the promise, we have the gift.

Faith that enables us to receive God's gifts is itself a gift, of which some measure is imparted to every human being. It grows as it is exercised in appropriating the Word of God. In order to strengthen faith, we must often bring it into contact with the Word.

In the study of the Bible the student should be led to see the power of God's word. In the creation, "He spoke, and it was done; He commanded, and it stood fast." He "calls those things which do not exist as though they did" (Ps. 33:9; Rom. 4:17), for when He calls them, they are.

The World's True Nobility

How often those who trusted the word of God have withstood the power of the whole world—Enoch, holding fast his faith in the triumph of righteousness against a corrupt and scoffing generation; Noah and his household against people of his time, men and women of the greatest physical and mental strength and the most debased in morals; the children of Israel at the Red Sea, a helpless, terrified multitude of slaves, against the mightiest army of the mightiest nation on the globe; David, a shepherd boy, having God's promise of the throne, against Saul, the established monarch, determined to hold fast his power; Shadrach and his companions in the fire, and Nebuchadnezzar on the throne; Daniel among the lions, his enemies in the high places of the kingdom; Jesus on the cross, and the Jewish priests and rulers forcing even the Roman governor to work their will; Paul in chains led to a criminal's death, Nero the despot of a world empire.

Such examples are found not only in the Bible but abound in every record of human progress. The Vaudois and the Huguenots, Wycliffe and Huss, Jerome and Luther, Tyndale and Knox, Zinzendorf and Wesley, with multitudes of others, have witnessed to the power of God's word against human power and policy in support of evil. These are the world's true nobility. This is its royal line. In this line young people of today are called to take their places.

Faith is needed in the smaller no less than in the greater experiences of life. In all our daily interests and occupations the sustaining strength of God becomes real to us through an abiding trust.

Viewed from its human side, life is an untried path. In regard to our deeper experiences, we each walk alone. Into our inner life no other human being can fully enter. As little children set forth on that journey, how earnest should be the effort to direct their trust to the sure Guide and Helper!

As a shield from temptation and an inspiration to purity and truth, no other influence can equal the sense of God's presence. "All things are naked and open to the eyes of Him to whom we must give account." He is "of purer eyes than to behold evil, and cannot look on wickedness." Heb. 4:13; Hab. 1:13. This thought was Joseph's shield amidst the corruptions of Egypt. To the allurements of temptation his answer was steadfast: "How . . . can I do this great wickedness, and sin against God?" Gen. 39:9. Faith, if cherished, will provide that shield to every soul.

Only the sense of God's presence can banish the fear that, for timid children, would make life a burden. Help them to fix in memory the promise, "The angel of the Lord encamps all around those who fear Him, and delivers them." Ps. 34:7. Have them read that wonderful story of Elisha in the mountain city, with a mighty encircling band of heavenly angels between him and the hosts of armed men. Tell them how God's angel appeared to Peter, in prison and condemned to death; how, past the armed guards, the massive doors and great iron gateway with their bolts and bars, the angel led God's servant forth in safety.

Picture for them that scene on the sea, when Paul the prisoner, on his way to trial and execution, spoke those grand words of courage and hope: "I urge you to take heart, for there will be no loss of life among you. . . . For there stood by me this night an angel of the God to whom I belong and whom I serve, saying, 'Do not be afraid, Paul; you must be brought before Caesar; and, indeed, God has granted you all those who sail with you.'" So, because there was in that ship one man through whom God could work, the whole shipload of heathen soldiers and sailors was preserved. "They all escaped safely to land." Acts 27:22-24, 44.

These things were written not merely that we might read and wonder, but that the same faith which worked in God's servants of old might work in us. In no less marked a manner than He worked then will He work now wherever there are hearts of faith to be channels of His power. Teach the self-distrustful, whose lack of self-reliance leads them to shrink from care and responsibility, to rely upon God. Thus many a person who otherwise would be but a cipher in the world, perhaps only a helpless burden, will be able to say with the apostle Paul, "I can do all things through Christ who strengthens me." Phil. 4:13.

God Is the Guardian of Right

For the child who is quick to resent injuries, faith has precious lessons. The disposition to resist evil or to avenge wrong is often prompted by a keen sense of justice and an active, energetic spirit. Children should be taught that God is the eternal guardian of right. He has a tender care for the beings whom He so loved as to give His dearest Beloved to save. He will deal with every wrongdoer.

"He who touches you touches the apple of His eye." Zech. 2:8. "Commit your way to the Lord, trust also in Him, and He shall bring it to pass. . . . He shall bring forth your righteousness as the light, and your justice as the noonday." Ps. 37:5, 6.

"Those who know Your name will put their trust in You; for You, Lord, have not forsaken those who seek You." Ps. 9:10.

The compassion that God manifests toward us, He tells us to manifest toward others. Encourage the impulsive, the self-sufficient, the revengeful, to behold the meek and lowly One, led as a lamb to the slaughter, unretaliating as a sheep before its shearers. Point them to Him whom our sins have pierced and our sorrows burdened, and they will learn to endure, to forbear, and to forgive.

Through faith in Christ every deficiency of character may be supplied, every defilement cleansed, every fault corrected, every excellence developed.

"You are complete in Him." Col. 2:10.

Prayer and faith are closely allied, and they need to be studied together. In the prayer of faith there is a divine science, a science that everyone who would make his or her lifework a success must understand. Christ says, "Whatever things you ask when you pray, believe that you receive them, and you will have them." Mark 11:24. He makes it plain that our asking must be according to God's will. We must ask for the things He has promised, and whatever we receive must be used in doing His will. When the conditions have been met, the promise is unequivocal.

For the pardon of sin, for the Holy Spirit, for a Christlike temper, for wisdom and strength to do His work, for any gift He has promised, we may ask; then we are to believe that we receive, and thank God that we have received. The gift is in the promise, and we may go about our work assured that the gift, which we already possess, will be realized when we need it most.

Prayer a Necessity
To live thus by the Word of God means the surrender to Him of the whole life. We will feel a continual sense of need and dependence, a draw-

ing out of the heart after God. Prayer is a necessity, for it is the life of the soul. Family prayer, public prayer, have their place, but it is secret communion with God that sustains the soul life.

In the mount with God Moses saw the pattern of that wonderful building which was to be the abiding place of His glory. It is in the mount with God—in the secret place of communion—that we are to contemplate His glorious ideal for humanity. Thus we shall be enabled so to fashion our character building that to us may be fulfilled His promise, "I will dwell in them and walk among them. I will be their God, and they shall be My people." 2 Cor. 6:16.

It was in hours of solitary prayer that Jesus received wisdom and power. Encourage the young to follow His example in finding at dawn and twilight a quiet season for communion with their Father in heaven. And throughout the day let them lift up their hearts to God. At every step of our way He says, "I the Lord your God will hold your right hand, . . . Fear not, I will help you." Isa. 41:13.

These are lessons that only people who have learned them can teach. It is because so many parents and teachers profess to believe the Word of God while their lives deny its power, that the teaching of Scripture has no greater effect on children and youth. It is one thing to treat the Bible as a book of good moral instruction, to be followed so far as is consistent with the spirit of the times and our position in the world, it is another thing to regard it as it really is—the Word of the living God, the Word that is our life, the Word that is to mold our actions, our words, and our thoughts. To hold God's Word as anything less than this is to reject it. And this rejection by those who profess to believe it, is foremost among the causes of skepticism and infidelity in today's youth.

Take Time With God

Unprecedented intensity is taking possession of the world. In amusement, in moneymaking, in the contest for power, in the very struggle for existence, there is a terrible force that engrosses body and mind and soul. In the midst of this maddening rush, God is speaking. He invites us to come apart and commune with Him. "Be still, and know that I am God." Ps. 46:10.

Many, even in their seasons of devotion, fail to receive the blessing of real communion with God. They are in too great haste. With hurried steps they press through the circle of Christ's loving presence, pausing perhaps a moment within the sacred precincts, but not waiting for counsel. They have no time to remain with the divine Teacher. With their burdens they return to their work.

These workers can never attain the highest success until they learn the secret of strength. They must give themselves time to think, to pray, to wait upon God for a renewal of physical, mental, and spiritual power. They need the uplifting influence of His Spirit. Receiving this, they will be quickened by fresh life. The wearied frame and tired brain will be refreshed, the burdened heart lightened.

Not just a pause for a moment in His presence, but personal contact with Christ—sitting down in companionship with Him—this is our need. What a great day it will be for the children of our homes and the students of our schools when parents and teachers learn in their own lives the precious experience pictured in these words by Solomon: "Like an apple tree among the trees of the woods, so is my beloved among the sons. I sat down in his shade with great delight, and his fruit was sweet to my taste. He brought me to the banqueting house, and his banner over me was love." Song of Solomon 2:3, 4.

Chapter 31

The Lifework

Success in any line demands a definite aim. People who achieve true success in life keep steadily in view the aim worthy of their endeavor. Such an aim is set before the young people of today. The Heaven-appointed purpose of giving the gospel to the world in this generation is the noblest that can appeal to any human being. It opens a field of effort to everyone whose heart Christ has touched.

God's purpose for the children growing up in our homes is wider, deeper, higher, than our restricted vision has comprehended. From the humblest lot those whom He has seen faithful have in times past been called to witness for Him in the world's highest places. And many a young person of today, growing up as did Daniel in his Judean home, studying God's Word and His works, and learning the lessons of faithful service, will stand in legislative assemblies, in halls of justice, or in royal courts, as a witness for the King of kings. Multitudes will be called to a wider ministry. The whole world is opening to the gospel.

Millions upon millions have never so much as heard of God or of His love revealed in Christ. It is their right to receive this knowledge. And it rests with us who have received the knowledge, with our children to whom we may impart it, to answer their cry. To every household and every school, to every parent, teacher, and child upon whom has shone the light of the gospel, comes at this crisis the question put to Esther the queen at that crisis in Israel's history: "Who knows whether *you* have come to the kingdom for such a time as this?" Esther 4:14.

The Suffering of God

Those who think of the result of hastening or hindering the gospel think of it in relation to themselves and to the world. Few think of its relation to God. Few give thought to the suffering that sin has caused our Creator. All heaven suffered in Christ's agony, but that suffering did not begin or end with His manifestation in humanity. The cross is a revelation to our dull senses of the pain that, from its very inception, sin has brought to the heart of God. Every departure from right, every deed of cruelty, every failure of humanity to reach God's ideal, brings grief to Him. When there came upon Israel the calamities that were the sure result of separation from God—persecution by their enemies, cruelty, and death—it is said that "His soul could no longer endure the misery of Israel." "In all their affliction He was afflicted." Judges 10:16; Isa. 63:9. As the "whole creation groans and labors with birth pangs" (Rom. 8:22), the heart of the infinite Father is pained in sympathy.

Our world is a vast gathering of sin-and-disease-stricken people, a scene of misery that we dare not allow even our thoughts to dwell upon. Yet God feels it all. In order to destroy sin and its results He gave His best Beloved, and He has put it in our power, through cooperation with Him, to bring this scene of misery to an end. "This gospel of the kingdom will be preached in all the world as a witness to all the nations; and then the end will come." Matt. 24:14.

"Go into all the world and preach the gospel to every creature" (Mark 16:15) is Christ's command to His followers. Not all are called to be ministers or missionaries in the ordinary sense of the term, but all may be workers with Him in giving the "glad tidings" to the world. To all, great or small, learned or ignorant, old or young, the command is given.

In view of this command, dare we educate our sons and daughters for only a life of respectable conventionality, a life professedly Christian but lacking His self-sacrifice, a life on which the verdict of Him who is truth must be, "I know you not"?

Thousands are doing this. They think to secure for their children the benefits of the gospel while they deny its spirit. But this cannot be. Those who reject the privilege of fellowship with Christ in service reject the only training that imparts a fitness for participation with Him in His glory. They reject the training that in this life gives strength and nobility of character. Many a father and mother, denying their children to the cross of Christ, have learned too late that they were thus giving them over to the enemy. They sealed their ruin not alone for the future but for the present life.

Even in seeking a preparation for God's service, many are turned aside by wrong methods of education. Life is too generally regarded as made up of distinct periods—the period of learning and the period of doing, of preparation and of achievement. In preparation for a life of service, young people are sent to school to acquire knowledge by the study of books. Cut off from the responsibilities of everyday life, they become absorbed in study and often lose sight of its purpose. The ardor of their early consecration dies out, and too many take up with some personal, selfish ambition.

Upon graduation, thousands find themselves out of touch with life. They have so long dealt with the abstract and theoretical that when the whole being must be roused to meet the sharp contests of real life, they are unprepared. Instead of the noble work they had purposed, their energies are engrossed in a struggle for mere subsistence. After repeated disappointments, in despair even of earning an honest livelihood, many drift into questionable or criminal practices. The world is robbed of the service it might have received, and God is robbed of the souls He longed to uplift, ennoble, and honor as representatives of Himself.

Human Judgment Faulty

Many parents err in discriminating between their children in the matter of education. They make almost any sacrifice to secure the best advantages for one that is bright and apt. But these opportunities are not considered necessary for those who are less promising. Little education is considered essential for the performance of life's ordinary duties.

But who is capable of selecting from a family of children the ones upon whom will rest the most important responsibilities? Remember the experience of Samuel when sent to anoint from the sons of Jesse one to be king over Israel. Seven noble-looking young men passed before him. As he looked at the first, in features handsome, in form well-developed, and in bearing princely, the prophet exclaimed, "Surely the Lord's anointed is now before the Lord." But God said, "Do not look on his appearance or on the height of his stature, because I have rejected him; for the Lord does not see as mortals see; they look on the outward appearance, but the Lord looks on the heart." So of all the seven the testimony was, "The Lord has not chosen any of these." 1 Sam. 16:6, 7, 10, NRSV. Not until David had been called from watching the flock was the prophet permitted to fulfill his mission.

The elder brothers, from whom Samuel would have chosen, did not possess the qualifications that God saw to be essential in a ruler of His people. Proud, self-centered, self-confident, they were set aside for the one whom they lightly regarded, one who had preserved the simplicity and sincerity of his youth, and who, while little in his own sight, could be trained by God for the responsibilities of the kingdom. So today, in many a child whom the parents would pass by, God sees capabilities far above those revealed by others who are thought to possess great promise.

And as regards life's possibilities, who is capable of deciding what is great and what is small? Many a worker in the lowly places of life, by setting on foot agencies for the blessing of the world, has achieved results that kings might envy!

Make certain, then, that every child receives an education for the highest service. "In the morning sow your seed, and in the evening do not withhold your hand; for you do not know which will prosper, either this or that." Eccl. 11:6.

The specific place appointed us in life is determined by our capabilities. Not all reach the same development or do the same work with equal efficiency. God does not expect the hyssop to attain the proportions of the cedar, or the olive the height of the stately palm. But each should aim just as high as the union of human with divine power makes possible.

Many do not become what they might because they do not put forth the power that is in them. They do not, as they might, lay hold on divine strength. Many are diverted from the line in which they might reach the truest success. Seeking greater honor or a more pleasing task, they attempt something for which they are not fitted. Many a person whose talents are adapted for some other calling is ambitious to enter a profession, and one who might have been successful as a farmer, an artisan, or a nurse, fills inadequately the position of a minister, a lawyer, or a physician. Others, who might have filled a responsible calling, for lack of energy, application, or perseverance, content themselves with an easier place.

We need to follow more closely God's plan of life. To do our best in the work that lies nearest, to commit our ways to God, and to watch for the indications of His providence—these are rules that ensure safe guidance in the choice of an occupation.

He who came from heaven to be our example spent nearly thirty years in common, mechanical work, but during this time He was studying the Word and the works of God. He also was helping and teaching all whom His influence could reach. When His public ministry began, He went about healing the sick, comforting the sorrowful, and preaching the gospel to the poor. This is the work of all His followers.

"The greatest among you," Christ said, "must become like the youngest, and the leader like one who serves. For . . . I am among you as one who serves." Luke 22:26, 27, NRSV.

Love and loyalty to Christ are the spring of all true service. In the heart touched by His love, there is born a desire to work for Him. This desire should be encouraged and rightly guided. Whether in the home, the neighborhood, or the school, the fact that there are poor, afflicted, ignorant, or unfortunate people should be regarded, not as a misfortune, but as affording a valuable opportunity for service.

In this work, as in every other, skill is gained in the work itself. It is by training in the common duties of life and in ministry to the needy and suffering, that efficiency is assured. Without this the best-meant efforts often are useless and even harmful. It is in water, not on the land, that people learn to swim.

Importance of Church Membership

Another obligation, too often lightly regarded—one that should be made plain to every young person who has been awakened to the claims of Christ—is the obligation of church relationship. Very close and sacred is the relation between Christ and His church—He the bridegroom, the church the bride; He the head, the church the body. Connection with Christ, then, involves connection with His church.

The church is organized for service, and in a life of service to Christ, connection with the church is one of the first steps. Loyalty to Christ demands the faithful performance of church duties. This is an important part of one's training, and in a church imbued with the Master's life it will lead directly to effort for the outside world.

There are many lines in which young people can find opportunity for helpful effort. Organize them into bands for Christian service. Parents and teachers, by taking an interest in their work, will be able to give them the benefit of their own larger experience, and can help them make their efforts effective for good.

Acquaintance awakens sympathy, and sympathy is the spring of effective ministry. To awaken in children and young people sympathy and the spirit of sacrifice for the suffering millions on other continents, let them become acquainted with these lands and their peoples. In this line much might be accomplished in our schools. Instead of dwelling on the exploits of the Alexanders and Napoleons of history, encourage students to study the lives of greats such as the apostle Paul, Martin Luther, Moffat, Livingstone, Carey, and the present global advances of missionary effort.

Young and Old Needed

In this closing work of the gospel there is a vast field to be occupied, and more than ever the work is to enlist helpers from the common people. Both young and old will be called from the farm, the vineyard, and the workshop, and sent forth by the Master to give His message. Many of these may have little education, but Christ sees in them qualifications that will enable them to fulfill His purpose. If they put their hearts into the work, and continue to be learners, He will fit them to work for Him. He who knows the depths of the world's misery and despair, knows by what means to bring relief. He sees on every hand souls in darkness, bowed down with sin, sorrow, and pain. But He also sees their possibilities. He sees the height to which they may attain.

The burden for these needy ones in the rough places of the earth Christ lays upon those who can feel for the ignorant and those who have wasted their talents. He will be present to help workers whose hearts are susceptible to pity. He will work through those who can see mercy in misery, and gain in loss. When the Light of the world passes by, calamities will be seen as disguised blessings; woes, as mercies. Workers from the common people, sharing the sorrows of fellow human beings as their Master shared the sorrows of the whole human race, will by faith see Him working with them.

"The great day of the Lord is near; it is near and hastens quickly."

Zeph. 1:14. And a world is to be warned.

With such preparation as they can gain, thousands upon thousands of people of all ages should be giving themselves to this work. Already many are responding to the call of the Master Worker, and their numbers will increase. Christian educators should give such workers sympathy and co-operation. They should encourage and assist students under their care to gain the preparation needed for service.

In no line of work can young people receive greater benefit. All who engage in ministry are God's helping hand. They are co-workers with the angels; rather, they are the human agencies through whom the angels accomplish their mission. Angels speak through their voices, and work by their hands. And the human workers, cooperating with heavenly agencies, have the benefit of their education and experience. As a means of education, what "university course" can equal this?

With such an army of workers as our youth, rightly trained, might furnish, how soon the message of a crucified, risen, and soon-coming Savior might be carried to the whole world! How soon might the end come—the end of suffering and sorrow and sin! How soon, in place of a possession here, with its blight of sin and pain, our children might receive their inheritance where "the righteous shall inherit the land, and dwell in it forever," where "the inhabitant will not say, 'I am sick,'" and "the voice of weeping shall no longer be heard." Ps. 37:29; Isa. 33:24; 65:19.

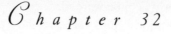

C h a p t e r 32

Preparation

The child's first teacher is its mother. During the period of greatest susceptibility and most rapid development the little one's education is to a great degree in her hands. To her first is given opportunity to mold the character for good or for evil. She should understand the value of her opportunity, and, above every other teacher, should be qualified to use it to the best account. Yet the one whose influence in education is most potent and far-reaching is the one on whom the least systematic effort is focused.

Too often those to whom the care of the little child is committed are ignorant of its physical needs. They know little of the laws of health or the principles of development. Nor are they better fitted to care for its mental and spiritual growth. They may be qualified to conduct business or to shine in society, they may have made creditable attainments in literature and science, but of the training of a child they have little knowledge. Chiefly because of this lack, especially because of the early neglect of physical development, a large proportion of the human race die in infancy, and of those who reach maturity many find life but a burden.

On fathers as well as mothers rests a responsibility for the child's earlier as well as its later training. For both parents the demand for thorough preparation is most urgent. Men and women should become acquainted with the laws of physical development—with physiology and hygiene, with the bearing of prenatal influences, with the laws of heredity, sanitation, dress, exercise, and the treatment of disease. They should also understand the laws of mental development and moral training.

The Infinite One has counted this work of education so important that messengers from His throne have been sent to a mother-to-be to answer the question, "How shall we order the child, and how shall we do unto him?" (Judges 13:12, KJV), and to instruct a father concerning the education of a promised son.

Training for Parenthood Needed

Never will education accomplish all that it might and should accomplish until the importance of the parents' work is fully recognized, and they receive a training for its sacred responsibilities.

The necessity of preparatory training for the teacher is universally admitted, but few recognize the character of the most essential preparation. Those who appreciate the responsibility involved in training children and youth will realize that instruction in scientific and literary lines alone cannot suffice. Teachers should have a more comprehensive education than can be gained by the study of books. They should possess not only strength but breadth of mind; they should be not only whole-souled but large-hearted.

Only He who created the mind and ordained its laws can perfectly understand its needs or direct its development. The principles of education that He has given are the only safe guide. A qualification essential for every teacher is a knowledge of these principles and such complete acceptance of them that they will be a controlling power in the life.

Experience in practical life is indispensable. Order, thoroughness, punctuality, self-control, evenness of disposition, self-sacrifice, integrity, and courtesy are essential qualifications.

Because there is so much cheapness of character, so much counterfeit today, it is more than ever necessary for the teachers' words, attitude, and deportment to represent the elevated and the true. Children are quick to detect affectation or any other weakness or defect. Teachers can gain the respect of their pupils in no other way than by revealing in their own characters the principles that they seek to teach. Only as they do this in their daily lives can they have a permanent influence for good on their students.

Health to Be Guarded

For almost every other qualification that contributes to success, teachers are in great degree dependent upon physical vigor. The better the health, the better will be the work accomplished.

So wearing are teachers' responsibilities that special effort on their part is required to preserve vigor and freshness. Often they become heart-weary and brain-weary, with the almost irresistible tendency to depression, coldness, or irritability. It is their duty not merely to resist such moods but to avoid their cause. They need to keep the heart pure, sweet, trustful, and sympathetic. In order to be always firm, calm, and cheerful, they must preserve the strength of brain and nerve.

Since quality is more important than quantity, teachers should guard against overwork— against attempting too much in their own line of duty, against accepting other responsibilities that would unfit them for their work, and against engaging in amusements and social pleasures that are exhausting rather than recuperative.

Outdoor exercise, especially in useful labor, is one of the best means of recreation for body and mind, and the example of teachers will inspire students with interest in, and respect for, manual labor.

In every line, teachers should scrupulously observe the principles of health. They should do this not only because of its bearing upon their own usefulness, but also because of its influence on their pupils. They should be temperate in all things. In diet, dress, work, and recreation, they are to set an example.

Physical health and uprightness of character should be combined with high literary qualifications. The more of true knowledge teachers have, the better will be their work. The schoolroom is no place for surface work. No teacher who is satisfied with superficial knowledge will attain a high degree of efficiency.

But the usefulness of teachers depends not so much on the actual amount of their acquirements as on the standard at which they aim. True teachers are not content with dull thoughts, an indolent mind, or a loose memory. They constantly seek higher attainments and better methods. In the work of true teachers there is a freshness, a quickening power, that awakens and inspires their pupils.

Teachers must have aptness for their work. They must have the wisdom and tact required to deal with minds. Teachers are needed who are quick to discern and improve every opportunity for doing good, teachers who combine enthusiasm with true dignity. Teachers are needed who are able to control, "apt to teach," teachers who can inspire thought, arouse energy, and impart courage and life.

Children and young people differ widely in disposition, habits, and training. Some have no definite purpose or fixed principles. They need to be awakened to their responsibilities and possibilities. Few children have been trained properly at home. Some have been household pets. Their whole training has been superficial. Allowed to follow inclination and to shun responsibility, they lack stability, perseverance, and self-denial. Often they regard all discipline as unnecessary. Others have been censured and discouraged, arbitrary restraint and harshness having developed in them obstinacy and defiance. If these deformed characters are to be reshaped, the work must, in most cases, be done by teachers.

To accomplish this successfully, they must have the sympathy and insight that will enable them to trace to their cause the faults and errors of their students. They also must have the tact, patience, and firmness that will enable them to impart to each the needed help. The vacillating and ease loving will need such encouragement and assistance to stimulate exertion. The discouraged will need sympathy and appreciation to create confidence and thus inspire effort.

Teachers often fail of coming sufficiently into social relation with their students. They manifest too little sympathy and tenderness, and too much of the dignity of the stern judge. While teachers must be firm and decided, they should not be exacting or dictatorial. Being harsh and censorious, standing aloof from their pupils or treating them indifferently, will close avenues to influence them for good.

Under no circumstances should teachers manifest partiality. To favor the bright, attractive pupil, and be critical, impatient, or unsympathetic toward those who most need encouragement and help, is to reveal a total misconception of the teacher's work. It is in dealing with faulty, trying ones that character is tested and it is proved whether teachers are really qualified for their work.

Great is the responsibility of those who take upon themselves the guidance of a human soul. True fathers and mothers count theirs a trust from which they can never be wholly released. Boys and girls from their earliest to their latest days feel the power of that tie which binds them to the parents' heart. The acts, the words, the very looks of the parents, continue to mold children for good or for evil. Teachers share this responsibility. They need constantly to realize its sacredness and to keep in view the purpose of their work. They are not merely to accomplish the daily tasks, to please their employers, and maintain the standing of the school, they also must consider the highest good of their students as individuals, the duties that life will lay on them, the service it requires, and the preparation demanded. The work that teachers do day by day will exert an influence on their pupils, and through them on others, that will extend and strengthen until time shall end. They must meet the fruits of this work in that great day when every word and deed shall be brought in review before God.

Teachers who realize this will not feel that their work is completed when they have finished the daily routine of recitations and their pupils go home. They will carry these children and youth on their hearts. How to secure for them the noblest standard of attainment will be their constant study and effort.

Aim High

Teachers who discern the opportunities and privileges of their work will allow nothing to stand in the way of earnest endeavor for self-improvement. They will spare no pains to reach the highest standard of excellence. All that they desire their students to become, they will themselves strive to be.

The deeper the sense of responsibility and the more earnest the effort for self- improvement, the more clearly will teachers perceive and the more keenly regret the defects that hinder their usefulness. As they see and feel the magnitude of the work, its difficulties and possibilities, often they will cry out, "Who is sufficient for these things?"

Dear teachers, as you consider your need of strength and guidance, I urge you to consider the promises of Him who is the wonderful

Counselor: "Call to Me, and I will answer you." "I will instruct you and teach you in the way you should go: I will guide you with My eye." Jer. 33:3; Ps. 32:8.

As the highest preparation for your work, I point you to the words, the life, the methods, of the Prince of teachers. Here is your true ideal. Behold it, dwell upon it, until the Spirit of the divine Teacher takes possession of your heart and life.

"Reflecting as a mirror the glory of the Lord," you will be "transformed into the same image." 2 Cor. 3:18. Reflect Him. This is the secret of power over your students.

Cooperation

In the formation of character, no other influences count so much as the influence of the home. The teacher's work should supplement that of the parents but is not to take its place. It should be the effort of parents and teachers to cooperate in all that concerns the well-being of the child.

The work of cooperation should begin with the father and mother in the home life. In the training of their children they have a joint responsibility, and it should be their constant endeavor to act together. They should yield themselves to God, seeking help from Him to sustain each other. Together they should teach their children to be true to God, true to principle, and thus true to themselves and to all with whom they are connected. With such training, children will not be a cause of disturbance or anxiety at school. They will be a support to their teachers, and an example and encouragement to other students.

Parents who give this training are not likely to be found criticizing the teacher. They feel that both the interest of their children and justice to the school demand that, so far as possible, they sustain and honor the one who shares their responsibility.

Many parents fail here. By their hasty, unfounded criticism the influence of the faithful, self-sacrificing teacher is often well-nigh destroyed.

Many parents whose children have been spoiled by indulgence leave to the teacher the unpleasant task of repairing their neglect. Then by their own course they make his or her task almost hopeless. Their criticism and censure of the school management encourages insubordination in the children and confirms them in wrong habits.

If criticism or suggestion in regard to the teacher's work becomes necessary, it should be made in private. If this proves ineffective, the matter should be referred to those responsible for the management of the school. Nothing should be said or done to weaken the children's respect for the one on whom their well-being in so great degree depends.

The parents' intimate knowledge both of the character of the children and of their physical peculiarities or infirmities, if shared with the teacher, is valuable. It is to be regretted that many fail to realize this. Most parents show little interest in either the teacher's qualifications, or in cooperating with him or her.

Since parents rarely acquaint themselves with the teacher, it is important that the teacher seek the acquaintance of parents. Teachers should visit in the homes of their students and gain a knowledge of the influences and surroundings where they live. By coming personally in touch with their homes and lives, teachers may strengthen the ties that bind them to their pupils and may learn how to deal more successfully with their different dispositions and temperaments.

As teachers interest themselves in the home education, they impart a double benefit. Many parents, absorbed in work and care, lose sight of their opportunities to influence for good the lives of their children. Teachers can do much to arouse these parents to their possibilities and privileges. Other parents feel a heavy sense of their responsibility to see that their children become good and useful men and women. Often the teacher can assist these parents in bearing their burden, and, by counseling together, both teacher and parents will be encouraged and strengthened.

The Principle of Cooperation

The principle of cooperation is invaluable in the home training of the young. From their earliest years children should be led to feel that they are a part of the home firm. Even the little ones should be trained to share in the daily work and should be made to feel that their help is needed and appreciated. The older ones should be their parents' assistants, entering into their plans and sharing their responsibilities. Let fathers and mothers show their children that they value their help, desire their confidence, and enjoy their companionship, and the children will respond. Not only will the parents' burden be lightened and the children receive a practical training of inestimable worth, there will be a strengthening of the home ties and a deepening of the very foundations of character.

Cooperation should be the spirit of the schoolroom, the law of its life. Teachers who gain the cooperation of their pupils secure an invaluable aid in maintaining order. By helping in the schoolroom many students whose restlessness leads to disorder and insubordination would find an outlet for their superfluous energy. Let the older assist the younger, the strong the weak, and, so far as possible, let all be called upon to do something in which they excel. This will encourage self-respect and a desire to be useful.

It would be helpful for young people, and for parents and teachers as well, to study the lesson of cooperation as taught in the Scriptures. Among its many illustrations notice the building of the tabernacle—that object lesson of character building in which all the people united, "everyone whose heart was stirred, and everyone whose spirit was willing." Exod. 35:21.

Read how the wall of Jerusalem was rebuilt by the returned captives in the midst of poverty, difficulty, and danger, the great task accomplished successfully because "the people had a mind to work." Neh. 4:6. Consider the part acted by the disciples in the Savior's miracle of feeding the multitude. The food multiplied in the hands of Christ, but the disciples received the loaves and gave to the waiting throng.

"We are members of one another." As everyone therefore "has received a gift, minister it to one another, as good stewards of the manifold grace of God." Eph. 4:25; 1 Peter 4:10.

The words written of the idol builders of old might well be adopted as a motto by character builders of today: "Everyone helped his neighbor; and said to his brother, Be of good courage!" Isa. 41:6.

Chapter 34

Discipline

One of the first lessons that children need to learn is the lesson of obedience. Before they are old enough to reason, they may be taught to obey. By gentle, persistent effort, the habit should be established. To a great degree this may prevent those later conflicts between will and authority that create alienation and bitterness toward parents and teachers, and too often resistance of all authority, human and divine.

The object of discipline is to train children for self-government. They should be taught self-reliance and self-control. As soon as they are able to understand, their reasoning powers should be enlisted on the side of obedience. Show them that obedience is right and reasonable. Help them see that disobedience leads to disaster and suffering. When God says "You shall not," He is, in love, warning us of the consequences of disobedience, in order to save us from harm and loss.

Help children see that parents and teachers are representatives of God, and that as they act in harmony with Him, their laws in the home and the school are also His. As children are to obey parents and teachers, they also are to obey God.

Right Use of the Will

To direct the child's development without hindering it by undue control should be the study of both parent and teacher. Too much management is as bad as too little. The effort to "break the will" of a child is a terrible mistake. While force may secure outward submission, the result with many children is a more determined rebellion of the heart. Even if the parent or teacher succeeds in gaining control, the outcome may be no less harmful to the child.

The discipline of a human being who has reached the years of intelligence should differ from the training of a dumb animal. The beast is taught only submission to its master. For the beast, the master is mind, judgment, and will. This method, sometimes employed in the training of children, makes them little more than automatons. Mind, will, conscience, are under the control of another.

It is not God's purpose that any human mind should be thus dominated. Those who weaken or destroy individuality assume a responsibility that can result only in evil. While under authority, children may appear like well-drilled soldiers, but when the control ceases, the character will be found to lack strength and steadfastness. Having never learned self-government, the young recognize no restraint except the requirement of parents or teacher. This removed, they do not know how to use their liberty, and often give themselves up to indulgence that proves their ruin.

Since the surrender of the will is much more difficult for some students than for others, teachers should make obedience to their requirements as easy as possible. The will should be guided and molded but not ignored or crushed. Save the strength of the will; in the battle of life it will be needed.

Children should understand the true force of the will. They should be led to see what a great responsibility is involved in this gift. The will is the governing power in a person, the power of decision, or choice. Every human being possessed of reason has power to choose the right. In every experience of life, God's word to us is, "Choose for yourselves this day whom you will serve." Josh. 24:15. Everyone may place his or her will on the side of the will of God. All may choose to obey Him, and by thus linking themselves with divine agencies may stand where nothing can force them to do evil. In every young person, every child, lies the power, by the help of God, to form a character of integrity and to live a life of usefulness.

Parents and teachers, who by such instruction train children to self-control, will be the most useful and permanently successful. To superficial observers their work may not be valued so highly as that of those who hold the mind and will of children under absolute authority, but in later years the result of the better method of training will be seen.

Wise educators, in dealing with students, will seek to encourage confidence and strengthen the sense of honor. Children and youth are benefitted by being trusted. Many—even little children—have a high sense of honor. All desire to be treated with confidence and respect, and this is their right. They should not be led to feel that they cannot go out or come in without being watched. Suspicion demoralizes, producing the very evils it seeks to prevent. Instead of watching continually, as if suspecting evil, teachers who are in touch with their pupils will discern the workings of the restless mind and will set to work influences that will counteract evil. Lead students to feel that they are trusted, and most will seek to prove themselves worthy of the trust.

On the same principle it is better to request than to command. Those thus addressed have opportunity to prove themselves loyal to right principles. Their obedience is the result of choice rather than compulsion.

Establishing and Enforcing Rules

The rules governing the schoolroom should, so far as possible, represent the voice of the school. Every principle involved in them should be explained to students so that they may be convinced of its justice. Thus they will feel a responsibility to see that the rules are obeyed.

Rules should be few and well considered, and, when once made, should be enforced. Whatever is found impossible to change, the mind learns to recognize and adapt to, but the possibility of indulgence induces desire, hope, and uncertainty. The results are restlessness, irritability, and insubordination.

Make it plain that the government of God knows no compromise with evil. Neither in the home nor in the school should disobedience be tolerated. No parent or teacher who has at heart the well-being of those under his or her care will compromise with the stubborn self-will that defies authority or resorts to subterfuge or evasion in order to escape obedience. It is not love but sentimentalism that treats wrongdoing lightly, endeavors to secure conformity by coaxing or bribes, and finally accepts some substitute in place of the thing required.

"Fools mock at sin." Prov. 14:9. We should beware of treating sin as a light thing. Terrible is its power over the wrongdoer. "The iniquities of the wicked ensnare them, and they are caught in the toils of their sin." Prov. 5:2, NRSV. The greatest wrong done to children or youth is to allow them to become fastened in the bondage of evil habit.

Young people have an inborn love of liberty; they desire freedom; and they need to understand that these inestimable blessings are to be enjoyed only in obedience to the law of God. This law is the preserver of true freedom and liberty. It points out and prohibits those things that degrade and enslave, and to the obedient it affords protection from the power of evil.

The psalmist says: "I will walk at liberty, for I seek Your precepts." "Your testimonies also are my delight and my counselors." Ps. 119:45, 24.

In our efforts to correct evil we should guard against a tendency to faultfinding or censure. Continual censure bewilders but does not reform. With many minds, and often those of the finest susceptibility, an atmosphere of unsympathetic criticism is fatal to effort. Flowers do not unfold under the breath of a blighting wind.

A child frequently censured for some special fault comes to regard that fault as his or her peculiarity, something it is useless to strive against. Thus are created discouragement and hopelessness, often concealed under an appearance of indifference or bravado.

The true object of reproof is gained only when wrongdoers are led to see their fault and the will is enlisted for its correction. When this is accomplished, point them to the source of pardon and power. Seek to preserve their self-respect and to inspire them with courage and hope.

This work is the nicest*, the most difficult, the most important ever committed to human beings. It requires the most delicate tact, the finest susceptibility, a knowledge of human nature, and a heaven-born faith and patience, willing to work, watch, and wait.

Self-control and Discipline

Those who desire to control others must first control themselves. To deal passionately with a child or youth will only arouse resentment. When parents or teachers become impatient and are in danger of speaking unwisely, let them remain silent. There is wonderful power in silence.

Teachers must expect to meet perverse dispositions and hard, unrepenting hearts, but in dealing with them should never forget that they themselves were once children in need of discipline. Even now, with all their advantages of age, education, and experience, they often err and are in need of mercy and forbearance. In training the young they should consider that they are dealing with those who have inclinations to evil similar to their own. Youth have almost everything to learn, and it is much more difficult for some to learn than for others. With students of this kind teachers should bear patiently, not censuring their ignorance but improving every opportunity to give them encouragement. With sensitive, nervous students they should deal very tenderly. A sense of their own imperfections should lead them constantly to manifest sympathy and forbearance toward those who also are struggling with difficulties.

The Savior's rule, "Do to others as you would have them do to you" (Luke 6:31, NRSV), should be the rule of all who undertake the training of children and youth. They are the younger members of the Lord's family, heirs with us of the grace of life. Christ's rule should be sacredly observed toward the slowest of comprehension, the youngest, the most blundering, and even toward the erring and rebellious.

This rule will lead teachers to avoid, so far as possible, making public the faults or errors of students. They will seek to avoid giving reproof or punishment in the presence of others. They will not expel students until every effort has been put forth for their reformation. But when it becomes evident that a student is receiving no personal benefit, that defiance or disregard of authority is tending to overthrow the government of the school, and that his or her influence is contaminating others, then expulsion becomes a necessity. Yet with many the disgrace of public expulsion would lead to utter recklessness and ruin. In most cases when removal is unavoidable, the matter need not be made public. By counsel and cooperation with the parents, let the teacher privately arrange for the student's withdrawal.

In this time of special danger for the young, temptations surround them on every hand. Every school should be a "city of refuge," a place where tempted youth, may be dealt with patiently and wisely. Teachers who understand their responsibilities will separate from their own hearts and lives everything that would prevent them from dealing successfully with the willful and disobedient. Love and tenderness, patience and self-control, will at all times be the law of their speech. Mercy and compassion will be blended with justice. When it is necessary to give reproof, their language will not be exaggerated, but humble. In gentleness they will set before wrongdoers their errors and help them to recover. Every true teacher will feel that it is better to err on the side of mercy than on the side of severity.

Many youth who are thought incorrigible are not so hard of heart as they appear. Many who are regarded as hopeless may be reclaimed by wise discipline. Often these are the ones who most readily melt under kindness. If teachers gain the confidence of tempted ones and recognize and develop the good in their characters, they can, in many cases, correct the evil without calling attention to it.

The divine Teacher bears with the erring through all their perversity. His love does not grow cold, His efforts to win them do not cease. With outstretched arms He waits to welcome again and again the erring, the rebellious, and even the apostate. His heart is touched with the helplessness of the little child subject to rough usage. The cry of human suffering never reaches His ear in vain. Though all are precious in His sight, the rough, sullen, stubborn dispositions draw most heavily on His sympathy and love, for He traces from cause to effect. The one who is most easily tempted, and is most inclined to err, is the special object of His solicitude.

Parents and teachers should cherish the attributes of Him who makes the cause of the afflicted, the suffering, and the tempted His own. They should have "compassion on those who are ignorant and going astray," since they also are "subject to weakness." Heb. 5:2. Jesus treats us far better than we deserve, and as He has treated us, so we are to treat others. The course of no parent or teacher is justifiable if it is different from that which the Savior would pursue under similar circumstances.

Meeting Life's Discipline

Beyond the discipline of the home and the school, all have to meet the stern discipline of life. How to meet this wisely is a lesson that should be made plain to every child and to every young person. It is true that God loves us, that He is working for our happiness, and that, if His law had always been obeyed, we would never have known suffering. It is no less true that, in this world, as the result of sin, suffering, trouble, and burdens come to every life. We should teach children and youth to meet bravely these troubles and burdens. We should give them sympathy but never foster self-pity. What they need is that which stimulates and strengthens rather than weakens.

This world is not a parade ground, it is a battlefield. All are called to endure hardness, as good soldiers. Let young people be taught that the true test of character is found in the willingness to bear burdens, to take the hard place, to do the work that needs to be done, though it bring no earthly recognition or reward.

The true way of dealing with trial is not by seeking to escape it but by transforming it. This applies to all discipline, the earlier as well as the later. The neglect of the child's earliest training, and the consequent strengthening of wrong tendencies, makes the succeeding education more difficult, and too often causes discipline to be a painful process. Painful it must be to the lower nature, crossing, as it does, the natural desires and inclinations, but the pain may be lost sight of in a higher joy.

Let children and youth be taught that every mistake, every fault, every difficulty, conquered, becomes a stepping-stone to better and higher things. Through such experiences all who have ever made life worth living have achieved success.

> "The heights by great men reached and kept
> Were not attained by sudden flight,
> But they, while their companions slept,
> Were toiling upward in the night."

> "We rise by things that are under our feet;
> By what we have mastered of good and gain;
> By the pride deposed and the passion slain,
> And the vanquished ills that we hourly meet."

We "do not look at the things which are seen, but at the things which are not seen. For the things which are seen are temporary, but the things which are not seen are eternal." 2 Cor. 4:18. The exchange we make in the denial of selfish desires and inclinations is an exchange of the worthless and transitory for the precious and enduring. This is not sacrifice, but infinite gain.

"Something better" is the watchword of education, the law of all true living. Whatever Christ asks us to renounce, He offers something better in its stead. Often young people cherish objects, pursuits, and pleasures that may not appear to be evil but that fall short of the highest good. Let them be directed to something better than display, ambition, or self-indulgence. Bring them into contact with truer beauty, with loftier principles, and with nobler lives. Point them to the One "altogether lovely." When once the gaze is fixed upon Him, the life finds its center. The youthful enthusiasm, generous devotion, and passionate ardor find here their true object. Duty becomes a delight and sacrifice a pleasure. To honor Christ, to become like Him, to work for Him, is life's highest ambition and greatest joy.

"The love of Christ compels us." 2 Cor. 5:14.

*Partial definition of *nice:* fastidious, refined, delicate, precise, discriminative; calling for great care, accuracy, tact; having high standards of conduct.

Chapter 35

The School
of the Hereafter

Heaven is a school, its field of study the universe, its teacher the Infinite One. A branch of this school was established in Eden, and, after the plan of redemption has accomplished its purpose, education will again be taken up in the Eden school.

"What no eye has seen, nor ear heard, nor the human heart conceived," . . . God has prepared for those who love Him." 1 Cor. 2:9, NRSV. Only through His Word can a knowledge of these things be gained, and even this affords but a partial revelation.

The prophet of Patmos thus describes the location of the school of the hereafter: "I saw a new heaven and a new earth, for the first heaven and the first earth had passed away. . . . Then I, John, saw the holy city, New Jerusalem, coming down out of heaven from God, prepared as a bride adorned for her husband." Rev. 21:1, 2. "The city had no need of the sun, or of the moon to shine in it, for the glory of God illuminated it, and the Lamb is its light." Rev. 21:23.

Between the school established in Eden at the beginning and the school of the hereafter there lies the whole compass of this world's history—the history of human transgression and suffering, of divine sacrifice, and of victory over death and sin. Not all the conditions of that first school of

Eden will be found in the school of the future life. No tree of knowledge of good and evil will afford opportunity for temptation. No tempter is there, no possibility of wrong. Every character has withstood the testing of evil, and none are longer susceptible to its power.

"To him who overcomes," Christ says, "I will give to eat from the tree of life, which is in the midst of the Paradise of God." Rev. 2:7. The gift of the tree of life in Eden was conditional, and it was finally withdrawn. But the gifts of the future life are absolute and eternal. The prophet sees the "river of water of life, clear as crystal, proceeding from the throne of God and of the Lamb." "And on this side of the river and on that was the tree of life." And "there shall be no more death, nor sorrow, nor crying; and there shall be no more pain: for the former things have passed away." Rev. 22:1; 22:2, RV; 21:4.

Restored to God's presence, the human race will again, as at the beginning, be taught of Him: "My people shall know My name; . . . they shall know in that day that I am He who speaks: 'Behold, it is I.' " Isa. 52:6.

There, when the veil that darkens our vision is removed, and our eyes see that world of beauty of which we now catch glimpses through the microscope; when we look on the glories of the heavens, now scanned afar through the telescope; when, the blight of sin removed, the whole earth shall appear in "the beauty of the Lord our God," what a field will be open to our study! Students of science may read the records of creation and discern no reminders of the law of evil. They may listen to the music of nature's voices and detect no note of wailing or undertone of sorrow.

There the Eden life will be lived, the life in garden and field. "They shall build houses and inhabit them; they shall plant vineyards, and eat their fruit. They shall not build, and another inhabit; they shall not plant and another eat; for as the days of a tree, so shall be the days of My people, and My elect shall long enjoy the work of their hands." Isa. 65:21, 22. There Adam and his descendants will be restored to their lost kingship, and the lower order of beings will again recognize their authority; the fierce will become gentle, and the timid trustful.

History of infinite scope and of wealth inexpressible will be open to the redeemed. Here, from the vantage ground of God's Word, students are afforded a view of the vast field of history and may gain some knowledge of the principles that govern the course of human events. But their vision is still clouded, and their knowledge incomplete. Not until they stand in the light of eternity will they see all things clearly.

Then will be opened before the redeemed the course of the great conflict that had its birth before time began, and that ends only when time shall cease. The history of the inception of sin; of fatal falsehood in its crooked working; of truth that, swerving not from its own straight lines, has met and conquered error—all will be made manifest. The veil that interposes between the visible and the invisible world will be drawn aside, and wonderful things will be revealed.

Ministry of Angels

Not until the providences of God are seen in the light of eternity shall we understand what we owe to the care and interposition of holy angels. Celestial beings have taken an active part in human life and business. They have appeared in garments that shone like lightning. They have come in human form, dressed like travelers. They have accepted the hospitality of human homes. They have acted as guides to lost travelers. They have defeated the robber's purpose and turned aside the stroke of the enemy.

Though the rulers of this world know it not, often in their councils angels have spoken. Human eyes have looked at them. Human ears have listened to their appeals. In the council hall and the court of justice, heavenly messengers have pleaded the cause of the persecuted and oppressed. They have defeated purposes and arrested evils that would have brought wrong and suffering to God's children. To students in the heavenly school, all this will be unfolded.

Every redeemed one will understand the ministry of angels in his or her own life. What will it be to hold converse with one's guardian angel and learn the history of divine interposition in the individual life, of heavenly cooperation in every work for humanity!

All the perplexities of life's experience will then be made plain. Where to us have appeared only confusion and disappointment, broken purposes and thwarted plans, will be seen a grand, overruling, victorious purpose, a divine harmony.

There all who have served with unselfish spirit will see the fruit of their labors. They will see the outworking of every right principle and noble act. Something of this we see here. But how little of the result of the world's most noble work is in this life manifest to the doer!

Parents and teachers lie down in their last sleep, their lifework seeming to have been in vain. They do not know that their faithfulness has unsealed springs of blessing that can never cease to flow. Only by faith they see the children they have trained become a benediction and an inspiration to the world, and the influence repeat itself a thousandfold.

Faithful workers send out into the world messages of strength and hope and courage, words that carry blessing to hearts in every land. But as they work in loneliness and obscurity they know little of the results. Men and women sow the seed from which, above their graves, others reap blessed harvests. They plant trees, that others may eat the fruit. They are content here to know that they have set in motion agencies for good. In the hereafter the action and reaction of all these will be seen.

Of every gift that God has bestowed, leading people to unselfish effort, a record is kept in heaven. To trace this in its wide-spreading lines, to meet those who by our efforts have been uplifted and ennobled, to see in their history the outworking of true principles—this will be one of the studies and rewards of the heavenly school.

Joys and Pursuits in Heaven
There we shall know even as also we are known. There the loves and sympathies that God has planted in the soul will find truest and sweetest exercise. The pure communion with holy beings, the harmonious social life with the blessed angels and with the faithful ones of all ages, the sacred fellowship that binds together "the whole family in heaven and earth"—all are among the experiences of the hereafter.

There will be music there, and song, such music and song as, except in the visions of God, no mortal ear has heard or mind conceived.

"As well the singers as the players on instruments shall be there." Ps. 87:7, KJV. "They shall lift up their voice, they shall sing." Isa. 24:14.

"For the Lord will comfort Zion, He will comfort all her waste places; He will make her wilderness like Eden, and her desert like the garden of the Lord; joy and gladness will be found in it, thanksgiving and the voice of melody." Isa. 51:3.

There every power will be developed, every capability increased. The grandest enterprises will be carried forward, the loftiest aspirations will be reached, the highest ambitions realized. And still there will arise new heights to surmount, new wonders to admire, new truths to comprehend, fresh objects to call forth the powers of body and mind and soul.

All the treasures of the universe will be open to the study of God's children. With unutterable delight we shall enter into the joy and wisdom of unfallen beings. We shall share the treasures gained through ages upon ages spent in contemplation of God's handiwork. And the years of eternity, as they roll, will continue to bring more glorious revelations. "Exceedingly abundantly above all that we ask or think" (Eph. 3:20) will be, forever and forever, the impartation of the gifts of God.

"His servants shall serve Him." Rev. 22:3. The life on earth is the beginning of the life in heaven. Education on earth is an initiation into the principles of heaven. The lifework here is a training for the lifework there. What we now are, in character and holy service, is the sure foreshadowing of what we shall be.

"The Son of man did not come to be served, but to serve." Matt. 20:28. Christ's work below is His work above, and our reward for working with Him in this world will be the greater power and wider privilege of working with Him in the world to come. " 'You are My witnesses,' says the Lord, 'that I am God.' " Isa. 43:12. This also we shall be in eternity.

Why was the great controversy permitted to continue throughout the ages? Why was Satan's existence not cut short at the outset of his rebellion? It was that the universe might be convinced of God's justice in His dealing with evil, that sin might receive eternal condemnation. In the plan of redemption there are heights and depths that eternity itself can never exhaust, marvels into which the angels desire to look. The redeemed only, of all created beings, have in their own experience known actual conflict with sin. They have identified with Christ, and, as even the angels could not do, have entered into the fellowship of His sufferings. Will they have no testimony as to the science of redemption—nothing that will be of worth to unfallen beings?

Even now, "to the principalities and powers in the heavenly places" is "made known through the church the manifold wisdom of God." And He "raised us up together, and made us sit together in the heavenly places in Christ Jesus, that in the ages to come He might show the exceeding riches of His grace in His kindness toward us in Christ Jesus." Eph. 3:10, RV; 2:6, 7.

"In His temple everyone says, 'Glory'" (Ps. 29:9), and the song that the ransomed ones will sing—the song of their experience—will declare the glory of God: "Great and marvelous are Your works, Lord God Almighty! just and true are Your ways, O King of the saints! Who shall not fear You, O Lord, and glorify Your name? for You alone are holy." Rev. 15:3, 4.

In our earthly, sin-restricted life, the greatest joy and the highest education are found in service. And in the future state, freed from the limitations of sinful humanity, we shall find our greatest joy and highest education in witnessing, and learning anew "the riches of the glory of this mystery," "which is Christ in you, the hope of glory." Col. 1:27.

"It has not yet been revealed what we shall be, but we know that when He is revealed, we shall be like Him, for we shall see Him as He is." 1 John 3:2.

Then, in that great multitude which no one can number, presented "faultless before the presence of His glory with exceeding joy" (Jude 24), the Son of God—He whose blood has redeemed us and whose life has taught us—"shall see the travail of His soul, and be satisfied." Isa. 53:11.